MEZCLA

RECIPES TO EXCITE

IXTA BELFRAGE

EBURY
PRESS

Photography
YUKI SUGIURA

Prop styling
JESS MURPHY

Book design
TEGAN HENDEL

CONTENTS

INT

DUCT

RO

ION

The word *mezcla* (not to be confused with the delicious drink mezcal) means 'mix', 'mixture', 'blend' or 'fusion' in Spanish. It's a beautiful word that has meaning in food and cooking, and also in music and art.

Within the context of this book, it's about mixing flavours and ingredients, but it also goes beyond that. It's about how my mixed heritage and upbringing has shaped the person that I am and, ultimately, the way that I cook.

There's inspiration from around the world in these pages, but this book is largely an ode to three incredible countries that taught me to love food: Italy, where I lived as a child; Brazil, where my mother is from; and Mexico, where my paternal grandfather lived. Three countries that I grew up travelling to, eating in, obsessing over – three countries whose cuisines and ingredients have come to overlap in my subconscious over time, leading me to create food that has been described as 'quintessentially Ixta'.

So, here's a little bit about my life so far, and how it's shaped the way I cook ...

From Italy, Brazil and Mexico, with love

My story begins halfway up a mountain in Tuscany. When I was young, my father's job was cultivating relationships with Italian wine producers, and so we moved to Tuscany when I was three.

We lived in the old servant quarters of a beautiful fifteenth-century villa, surrounded by rolling Tuscan hills, vineyards and olive groves as far as the eye could see. My sister and I spent our days roaming the countryside with our dog, Giacomino, and life was pretty damn good.

I quickly became best friends with a girl I met at school, Giuditta, whose family changed my life by introducing me to the best Tuscan food, which is arguably the best food (along with Mexican and Brazilian food, but we'll get to that). Giuditta's uncle was the chef-owner of a restaurant called La Casellina, which served dishes that I came to fall madly in love with. Dishes like chicken liver *crostini*, tagliatelle with duck ragù, ravioli with *crema di rucola*, *fritto misto* of rabbit, courgette flowers and sage leaves and so much more ... Giuditta's grandfather, Ferruccio, used to make all the pasta for La Casellina in the laundry room of their family house, so whenever I went over, I would hang out with Ferruccio and watch him make pasta. I'll forever associate the smell of clean laundry with fresh pasta.

I am forever grateful for this beautiful part of the world where I spent my formative childhood years, the only place I feel truly at home. In the summer, the air is heady with the smell of ripe fruit, cypress trees, dust and grass. The sun shines brighter and time goes faster and slower all at once. The air is thick, dry and hot but, somehow, so much easier to breathe. I am not Italian, and in the grand scheme of my life so far, I didn't live there very long, and yet deep in my bones I feel that this mountain in Tuscany, more than anywhere else, is home.

The Brazilian influence comes from my mother, who is from Natal, in the north-east of the country. We visited many times when I was growing up, and I lived in Rio de Janeiro for a year when I was nineteen, one of the best years of my life and the last time I remember having absolutely no worries. I woke up to eat, go to the beach, drink and party, and slept just so I could do it all over again. It will come as no surprise that what I love most about Brazil is the food. I could write a whole book about my experience of the food in Brazil, but I need to condense my feelings to just a few paragraphs, so I'll tell you about one of my death row meals (of course, there is more than one).

When we used to visit my mother's home town, we would stay near Ponta Negra beach. It was idyllic, peppered with palm trees, and punctuated by Morro do Careca, an enormous and majestic sand dune down which people happily plunge all day. The beach was home to a few fish restaurants, and we had a favourite, of course, a rudimentary shack in the sand, the tables of which were close enough to the sea that the water would lap around your bare feet as the tide came in and the meal stretched into the late afternoon. Plastic tables were first loaded with *moqueca* (seafood stew), *pirão* (a sort of porridge made by beating hot seafood stock into coarse cassava flour), *macaxeira frita* (fried cassava chips) and an endless flow of guarana and caipirinhas. Next came whole fish and giant prawns, pulled fresh from the sea in front of our eyes and grilled next to our table. This was the meal of dreams.

Brazil holds a very special place in my heart, and you'll see its influence throughout these pages.

My father was born in the US to English parents. He grew up in the Bronx, an avid Yankee fan, during the McCarthy era. When he was fourteen, his father was accused of being a communist (he had been for a time, and still held allegiances) and was deported.

This might seem irrelevant, but the fact that my grandfather was deported from the US led him to settle in Mexico, where he spent thirty-five years of his life in a beautiful house in Cuernavaca, just outside Mexico City. Along with his wife, Mary, he ran this as a halfway house for political refugees, a halfway house where my mother and her family would find safety in '66, having fled from the Brazilian right-wing military regime.

From the garden of this house in Cuernavaca you can see the volcano Ixtaccíhuatl (sometimes spelled Iztaccíhuatl), which is my namesake and explains my affinity for volcanoes. My parents first met in my grandfather's garden in Cuernavaca (although they didn't end up together until decades later) and that's how I ended up with my name, although luckily they dropped the 'ccíhuatl' and just called me Ixta.

Because of all this, Mexico was also a huge part of my upbringing. I have never lived in Mexico (a fact I will one day correct), nor do I have Mexican blood, but it is very close to my heart. The country and its food feel like a part of my identity. I felt this connection before I ever went there, most likely because of my Mexican name, but also undoubtedly because of the significance of the country as a place of political refuge for both sides of my family.

When we visited my grandparents' house, there was nowhere I wanted to be more than the kitchen. It was quintessentially Mexican: decorated with tiles, terracotta and concrete in shades of deserts and sunsets. Their cooks were Gumer and Maria Concha, two short ladies with long grey hair, the kindest eyes and the widest smiles. By the time I met them, they had been cooking for my grandparents for twenty years. I hung at their elbows, marvelling at their speed and skill in stuffing and frying my favourite *chiles rellenos* (stuffed peppers), rolling corn tortillas and pounding chillies and spices for moles and salsas in a huge *molcajete* (pestle and mortar) made from volcanic rock. Made from a little piece of Ixtaccíhuatl, I always liked to think.

Growing up, I always found myself in the kitchen. Watching. Learning. Little did I know that I was soaking up food traditions like a sponge, because when I started cooking at a young age, having never been properly taught, it all just came naturally, like muscle memory from a past life.

The Ottolenghi effect

Fast forward twenty-six years from when I first picked up a knife and I'm writing this book. I've recently come from working in the Ottolenghi Test Kitchen, where I was given the freedom to flex my creativity, the guidance to learn how to write recipes and cookbooks and, ultimately, the encouragement to build my own identity. I am indebted and forever grateful to the man you all know as Ottolenghi and the man we at the Test Kitchen knew as Big Y. An incredibly kind, wise and fiercely intelligent man who has completely changed my life (and undoubtedly many of your lives too, through the language of food).

It wouldn't make sense for this book not to mention Yotam Ottolenghi, who influenced my cooking long before I ever met him. There are countless recipes in this book that simply wouldn't be there were it not for the fact that Yotam revolutionised the way we all cook, and the fact that by some inexplicable stroke of luck, I landed in his Test Kitchen all those years ago.

I worked for Yotam Ottolenghi for five years, first at NOPI restaurant and then at the OTK (Ottolenghi Test Kitchen), and I couldn't have asked for a better boss. He was always generous with his knowledge and selfless in his desire for others around him to succeed.

'Ottolenghi' is synonymous with food that is full of flavour, bursting with herbs, spices, chilli and citrus. It's vegetable-heavy and is often just as much of a joy to look at as it is to eat. It is considered but not fussy. Rustic but not slapdash. It takes inspiration from all over the world. This is the blueprint from which so many cooks these days work, myself very much included, and you will see his influence peppered throughout these pages.

Food for thought

I have been obsessed with food since I had conscious thought. I am forever grateful for a childhood that involved travelling extensively around Italy, Brazil and Mexico. I do not take this privilege for granted and I know that I wouldn't be writing this if it weren't for those experiences.

As I've said before, this book is, in many ways, an ode to those three countries that made me fall in love with food and that shaped me as a person and as a cook. But it's not only about them. My time at the Ottolenghi Test Kitchen, coupled with the effect of living in a world where culinary ideas can be shared in the time it takes to refresh your phone screen, mean that of course my sources of inspiration go far beyond those three countries.

You'll find recipes in this book that are twists on classics with traceable origins. More often than not, however, you'll find recipes that are unapologetically fusion. Recipes that are inspired by an eclectic *mezcla* of cuisines and cultures.

Since no one has come up with a better word to describe food that crosses cultures and transcends borders, let's just embrace that word: *FUSION!* Better yet, let's celebrate it. After all, most recipes were probably considered fusion before they became defining classics.

With the commitment to cooking fusion comes the responsibility of doing so considerately and respectfully. I always say the world would be a very boring place if we were only allowed to cook from, or be inspired by, our own culture; however, I am aware that this opinion comes from a position of great privilege. I have a mixed heritage and thus have always felt like a bit of a global citizen with no concrete notion of 'home', but I do not live with the devastating aftermath of appropriation. I am lucky. I recognise the privilege I live with and the opportunities I have been given.

I am inspired by cuisines from *all* over the world. I am an expert in *none* of them. None of the recipes in this book should be considered as an attempt to recreate traditions that I'm not versed in. These recipes celebrate how different cultures inspire my cooking, and how it would be nothing without that inspiration.

About this book

To help you navigate this book, I've divided the recipes into two main sections: **EVERYDAY** (quicker, easier recipes) and **ENTERTAINING** (longer recipes that require more time and ingredients). This means that you can easily flip to the kind of recipe you have the energy to achieve at any given time.

Within those sections, the recipes are further divided into **VEG**, **FISH** and **MEAT**, heavily weighted towards **VEG** (in fact, 60% of the recipes are veg) and the majority of those easily veganized, because, well, we're all trying to eat less meat and fish these days, aren't we? Besides that, *Ottolenghi Flavour* was definitive proof that vegetables can steal the show.

EVERYDAY consists of achievable dishes that don't skimp on flavour. These recipes are designed for when you need something great on the table,

fast. They are either short on time, equipment or ingredients and often come together in just one pot or tray. They could be described as 'midweek meals', although the concept of the working week means different things to different people.

ENTERTAINING consists of longer recipes to take your time over, for the love of cooking. Just to be clear, I'm not talking about the kind of entertaining that involves aprons and fluffed-up cushions. I'm talking about entertaining in the truest sense of the word. These are the recipes to experiment with when you have the time to slow down and really savour the process of cooking. Whether you're cooking for a crowd or for yourself is less important – it's about being in the mindset where you can enjoy the journey as well as the result.

Having said that, no one's stopping you cooking a recipe from **ENTERTAINING** on a Monday night after work, and by all means cook an **EVERYDAY** recipe on a Saturday afternoon for friends. Only you will know whether you're in the mood for something quick and easy, or for something more challenging, and these sections will help you pick the right recipe for that mood.

And then of course there's **THE END**, because all good things must come to an end. This is where you'll find some sweetness to soften the blow. Recipes are divided again by time and effort. **QUICK FIXES** are desserts that you can get on the table in (next to) no time. **SHOWSTOPPERS** are desserts that might need a little more love and attention.

From shorter midweek recipes to more adventurous projects, there are options for every mood within these pages. I hope you'll find plenty of recipes to cook over and over again, to get to know like the back of your hand and to make your own.

INGREDIENTS

Below is a list of some of my favourite ingredients that capture the spirit of **MEZCLA**. Some you will be familiar with, some maybe less so. All of them deserve a place on your shelf.

Azeite de dendê (red palm fruit oil) is an unrefined oil made from the pulp of the palm fruit. It's native to West Africa but ubiquitous in Brazilian cuisine, due to the movement of ingredients during the slave trade (4.9 million enslaved people were forcibly taken to Brazil). Its use as an unrefined cooking oil long predates its use as a commercial, refined and environmentally problematic oil. The unrefined cooking oil is very different to the refined, commercial oil, but it's still very important to make sure the brand you're using is fairtrade and RSPO (Roundtable of Sustainable Palm Oil) certified.

Azeite de dendê is one of my favourite ingredients: its flavour is unique, sort of like ghee spiked with carrot and paprika, but also nothing like that at all. It's a bright orangey-red, with an unmistakable aroma which makes two of my all-time favourite dishes – *moqueca* (a Brazilian seafood stew) and *pirão* (a Brazilian porridge of sorts, made by beating coarse cassava flour into hot seafood stock) – so special. Both these dishes are said to have originated with indigenous Brazilians, but were enhanced by enslaved people from Africa who permeated Brazilian cooking with African soul. You can find red palm fruit oil in Brazilian, West African and Caribbean speciality shops or online. Ghee or butter mixed with mild paprika can be used as a substitute.

Chillies I'm a huge fan of chillies and use them – perhaps excessively – throughout this book. That's not to say that you need to love chillies to cook from this book, so please don't skip over a recipe if it contains chilli. Chillies are optional throughout, and I guarantee that these recipes will still have tons of flavour if you omit them, or add less to your taste.

Habanero, Scotch bonnet, chipotle and Calabrian chillies are all very hot. If you come across these

in a recipe and don't like heat, omit them or try experimenting with milder options, to taste: fresh deseeded mild chillies, regular dried chilli flakes, Urfa chilli flakes. If you want flavour but none of the heat, try subbing chillies with red bell pepper flakes or mild paprika.

Ancho and cascabel chillies have medium-mild levels of heat, especially when deseeded, so these can also be experimented with in place of hotter chillies.

If you don't like chillies but want something punchy to stir into dishes like the mussels on page 99, simply mix together 150g of grated tomato, half a finely grated garlic clove, 1 teaspoon of lemon juice and ⅛ teaspoon of salt.

Calabrian chilli paste aka *crema di pepperoncino* is a bright red, textured condiment made from finely chopped Calabrian chillies, olive oil, salt and sometimes garlic. It's medium-hot, with a fruity, tangy kick similar(ish) to Scotch bonnet. A small spoonful stirred into soups, stews and sauces will completely enhance them. You can find it in Italian delis, speciality grocers and online. Alternatively, use the Scotch bonnet salsa recipe on page 31.

Habanero chillies are native to the Peruvian Amazon but are widely considered to be Mexican chillies. Throughout this book I use dried habaneros rather than fresh, which I've never come across in the UK. Dried habaneros are small, shrivelled and a dark reddy-brown colour. They have a very similar flavour to Scotch bonnet chillies, both being fruity and smoky; however, their being dried makes for a more intense experience, as the flavours are concentrated. Habaneros are my all-time favourite chilli, and sniffing a bag of them is a euphoric, catnip-like sensory experience for me. Habaneros are extremely hot, but they can also impart medium/mild heat and lots of flavour if they remain whole and unpierced. For mild heat, add them whole to sauces and try not to squash them at all during the cooking process. To impart a medium heat, squeeze them with the back of a spoon during cooking. If you enjoy excessive heat like me, you can chop them up, which will release the intense heat from the pith and seeds. I'd recommend adding chopped habanero in stages and tasting as you go. For even more flavour, char your habaneros in a very hot pan for a few minutes before cooking with them. You can find dried habaneros in many supermarkets, in Mexican grocers and online. Charred Scotch bonnet chillies can be used as an alternative.

Scotch bonnet chillies are ubiquitous in Caribbean and West African cuisine. They are very hot, with a fruity, tangy kick. Much like habaneros, their flavour can be harnessed without too much heat if they remain whole and unpierced, as their heat lies within the pith. Add them whole to stews, sauces, soups; the longer you leave them in, the more flavour/heat they will impart, as they soften during cooking. For medium-hot heat, squash them with the back of a spoon before removing them from whatever you're cooking. For intense heat, chop them up and add a little at a time, tasting as you go.

Scotch bonnets will vary in heat from one to another, so always taste as you go. You can find them in most greengrocers and in West African and Caribbean shops.

Cassava/macaxeira In Brazil, the root most commonly known around the world as cassava goes by many other names – *aipim, yuca, mandioca, macaxeira* – depending on where you're from. My mum is from Natal, in the north-east of Brazil, where it's called *macaxeira*, so that's what I've always called it. Cassava is native to Brazil and is incredibly versatile: the root is usually boiled or (boiled then) fried, in which case it has a vaguely similar texture to potato, but with a sweeter and slightly nutty flavour. The root can also be processed into starch or flour. Cassava has a thick, woody brown skin; you'll need a sharp peeler or knife to remove it, as well as the pink layer of flesh

beneath it. Once peeled, the flesh should be hard and white. If it's soft, with brown patches or black spots, you shouldn't use it. A dry, fibrous root runs through the centre of the cassava, which is easiest to remove once boiled. You can find cassava in some greengrocers and in West African, Caribbean and Brazilian shops. Use golden sweet potato or regular potatoes as an alternative.

Coconut milk doesn't need an explanation, but it's worth noting that whenever I call for coconut milk, I mean the type from a tin (that you'd use to make coconut-based curries, for example), not from a carton (that you'd use in coffee or cereal). I only ever use full-fat coconut milk with a minimum of 70% coconut extract (preferably 75%) and I encourage you to do the same. This info should be first on the ingredients list on the back of the tin. Make sure you whisk the contents of the tin together until smooth before measuring, as coconut milk will often separate into solid fat and liquid when it sits in a tin for too long, especially during colder months.

Creamed coconut is not the same as coconut cream. In the UK it usually comes in a small, 200g cardboard box, sometimes in a jar, but never in a tin. Creamed coconut is made from the dehydrated pulp of coconut and therefore is textured, sweet and intensely coconutty. If you mixed together desiccated coconut, coconut cream and coconut oil, you'd have something close to the texture and taste of creamed coconut. Unless the weather is hot, creamed coconut will solidify into a hard block, in which case you'll need to very gently heat it, so you can recombine the solids and fat. Tropical Sun 100% pure creamed coconut is the best of the best.

Dried porcini mushrooms are an incredibly powerful ingredient, full of meaty texture and concentrated umami flavour. They are widely used in Italian and especially Tuscan cooking, which is where I fell in love with them. Dried mixed wild mushrooms usually contain some porcini, so they are a good alternative. Dried shiitake have a completely different flavour profile, so should only be used at a push.

Ghee/clarified butter is most notably used in South Asian cuisine; however, I came to know and cook with it in Brazil, where it's called *manteiga da garrafa*, which roughly translates as 'bottle butter', so called because of its liquid state in the heat. Ghee or *manteiga da garrafa* is clarified butter, made by melting butter so the milk solids can be removed. This makes it easier to digest (as it has a lower lactose content) and also means that it can be kept at room temperature without spoiling (which is why it's a staple in many hot countries). Most importantly, the flavour is incredible and so much better than butter; it's savoury without being salty, slightly cheesy and has notes of caramel.

As a rule, avoid ghee that comes in a green and gold tin, which I find has a curious and overpowering smell of bubblegum. Go for ghee in a glass jar, if you can – Happy Butter Ghee is my go-to brand in the UK and is made from the milk of organic grass-fed cows. Alternatively, make your own! Melt good-quality butter over a low heat in a silver-coloured pan (this is so you can see the bottom). After about 5 minutes, the butter will begin to foam and after about 10 minutes the foam should disappear completely. Once the foam has gone and the solids at the bottom of the pan are golden-brown, remove from the heat. Strain the clarified butter through a sieve lined with kitchen paper, into a clean glass jar. Store at room temperature for a few months or refrigerate for up to 6 months. You can find ghee in most supermarkets and health food shops. Butter can be used as an alternative, and if you're vegan, use vegan ghee, vegan butter or olive oil.

Maple syrup needs no explanation. I simply want to acknowledge here that I use it a *lot* because I know I'm going to get pushback on it, as it's much more expensive than sugar. There are two main reasons I use maple syrup over sugar most of the time.

1. Superior flavour. I can't think of any other way to describe it than mapley and totally delicious, so I'll leave it at that. Odds are you don't need me to tell you what it tastes like.

2. It's a liquid, so there's no need to melt or dissolve it. This is handy in many recipes and especially when making caramels (pages 238, 261) because you can skip the part where you melt the sugar (a step I always manage to screw up).

I buy it online by the litre, which is much cheaper than buying lots of small bottles, and also necessary if you go through it at the rate that I do. You can absolutely use runny honey or sugar if you prefer.

Miso is a Japanese seasoning made from fermented soya beans. I tend to use a white miso paste by Miso Tasty, which is the perfect balance of sweet and savoury. Miso is the embodiment of umami, and therefore it can be used in so many contexts apart from Japanese or East Asian cuisine and it still makes perfect sense. I use it to make caramel (page 261) and in a butter that gets spooned all over lamb (page 219).

Plantain My mother, a Brazilian who grew up in Cuba, is obsessed with plantain. She grew up eating them alongside pretty much every meal, and brought my sister and me up in the same way, so now my fruit bowl is almost never without a couple of blackening plantains. Plantains are similar to bananas, except they are much larger and need to be cooked. They are most notably used in South American, Latin American, Caribbean and West African cooking, although they are native to South-east Asia. There is a plantain recipe for every stage of ripeness, from hard and green to soft and black. All the recipes in this book call for very ripe plantain; they should be soft, nearly all black, with only some yellow marks. You can get plantain at most greengrocers, and in West African or Caribbean shops.

Other things to note

Liquids in grams You'll probably notice that I measure pretty much anything over 4 tablespoons in grams, even liquids. This is because I find it easier to weigh ingredients straight into a bowl on a set of scales, rather than pouring them into a measuring jug and eyeballing how many millilitres they are. If you prefer using measuring jugs/cups, you absolutely can, just use the same amount in millilitres as I've specified in grams. This may not be technically correct, as some liquids have different volume, but it will be more or less the right amount. I gave up on thinking recipes can be followed precisely a long time ago. There should always be room for a margin of difference, for creativity, for winging it! We're all cooking on different stovetops, in different-sized pans, in ovens that function differently. Some of you are measuring ingredients, some of you aren't. Some of you are substituting ingredients or leaving some out. That's all absolutely fine!

Olive oil As a general rule, I use a milder (often slightly cheaper) extra virgin olive oil for cooking, and a stronger, peppery extra virgin olive oil to finish dishes with. I've referred to 'olive oil' throughout the book as I don't want to assume you also always have two types of olive oil on the go, but if you do, keep the peppery, more expensive stuff raw for drizzling with, and use the milder stuff to cook with.

Salt I use fine sea salt to cook with and flaked sea salt to finish dishes with. Stick to sea salt if you can; it's much better for you and doesn't have the chemical taste of iodised salt. Flaked sea salt has twice the volume of fine sea salt, so for example if I call for ½ teaspoon of flaked sea salt and you only have fine salt, use ¼ teaspoon.

Stock When I call for 'stock' in my recipes, whether that's veg, chicken or beef stock, I always mean liquid stock, rather than stock cubes (which I avoid). I assume stock is unsalted/unseasoned, but if yours isn't, adjust the seasoning in the rest of the dish. I also count bone broth as stock, so feel free to use that instead.

Kitchen tools

Blowtorches are not just for 'professionals'. Everyone should have one! They're incredibly useful when you want to achieve the kind of char that a home oven simply can't. I use one in recipes throughout this book: to crisp up mackerel skin (page 207), to char pieces of corn on cornbread (page 153), and to brûlée custard (page 275).

Food processor I'll admit this one is a bit of a luxury, but it's highly recommended if you cook a lot and enjoy cutting corners like me. A 10-minute chopping job can easily be reduced to 2 minutes with a food processor and the pulse mode.

Mandolins have a bad rep for being dangerous, but they're no more dangerous than a sharp knife if you're paying attention and being careful. A mandolin is brilliant for achieving thin, even slices, which are especially useful for gratins and salads.

Microplane I use my fine Microplane all the time, for everything from zesting lemons to grating Parmesan. My favourite use for a Microplane is for finely grating garlic (no need to remove the skin!). I always specify 'crushed/finely grated' garlic in the ingredients list as a nod to the fact that most people probably use garlic crushers, but I don't. Try grating an unpeeled garlic clove on a fine Microplane and you'll never look back.

Stand mixer Once again, this is a luxury and I certainly wouldn't encourage you to get one unless you're going to use it a lot. I use it to knead dough (which can easily be done by hand), but more importantly for making ice cream – both the Coffee ice cream (page 266) and the Miso caramel ice cream bomba (page 261) require a stand mixer.

E V E
D A

When it comes to cooking, I have two moods, and I'll bet that most of you do, too. Sometimes I'm so tired or bored of cooking that I just need something on the table, fast (continue to next paragraph), and sometimes I revel in the idea of a long, lazy afternoon of cooking (turn to page 122).

This section – **EVERYDAY** – is for the former, and when I'm in that mood, I love to cut corners. I get excited about finding better, quicker ways of doing things. Take, for example, the Porcini ragù on page 26. This recipe is inspired by the Spicy mushroom ragù from *Ottolenghi Flavour*, which I'm so pleased you all loved, but admittedly takes a million years to make. This porcini ragù has all the intensity of a ragù that has simmered for hours, but only takes 20 minutes from start to finish. Make it to believe it!

I'll say it loud and proud: I can be a little lazy. I don't think there's any shame in that. Considering how many hours I've spent in the kitchen, which would probably amount to months if not years if I added them up, you'll understand that when I find an easier way of getting great results, I get excited about it. Perhaps lazy is not the right word, and makes me sound like I don't care (believe me, I care!), so let's use the word thrifty instead. I'm thrifty with my time, with my ingredients (sometimes), with how many pans and bowls I am willing to wash up. Food processors, mandolins, Microplanes and stand mixers are my friends, and if I can use them to do a job in one minute that would otherwise take me ten, you better believe I'm going to use them.

This is good news for you, because it means I've come up with a rotation of achievable dishes for when you need something great on the table, fast. They are short on time or ingredients (or both) and big on flavour. They often come together in just one pot or tray.

PSA: I think it's worth noting that none of these recipes will come together in 10 minutes with only a handful of ingredients. There's absolutely nothing wrong with recipes like that – believe me, I'm often so tired of cooking that dinner is just tinned mackerel on toast – but this isn't that type of book. The recipes in this section are, by my standards, quicker, but not so much that they could be featured in a book about 10-minute meals. This book celebrates exciting ingredients and techniques, and I hope that you've picked it up because you're looking for something a bit different.

VEG

Cheesy roasted aubergines with salsa roja

3 medium aubergines, halved
    lengthways (900g)

3 tablespoons olive oil, plus extra to serve

¾ teaspoon fine salt

Salsa roja

2 tablespoons olive oil

15g unsalted butter

1 medium onion, peeled and
    finely chopped (120g)

2 cloves of garlic, finely grated/crushed

300g sweet, ripe cherry tomatoes

½ dried ancho chilli

1 dried habanero chilli (or a
    pinch of regular chilli flakes,
    if you prefer milder heat)

1 teaspoon cumin seeds

½ teaspoon coriander seeds

1 teaspoon fine salt

110g water

2 teaspoons tomato purée/paste

Cheese mix

25g feta, crumbled

25g Gruyère, roughly grated

100g mozzarella, drained well
    and torn into small pieces

100g double cream

Make ahead

The salsa roja will keep for up to a week
in the fridge.

Notes

Don't be afraid of the heat of the
habanero in the sauce – if it remains whole
and unpierced, it will impart only a fruity,
mild/medium heat. Squeeze it with the
back of a spoon to release more flavour
before removing it for medium/hot heat.
If, like me, you enjoy excessive heat, you
can blend it in. I recommend starting with
a quarter of the chilli, then blending and
tasting before adding more.

Inspired by *melanzane alla Parmigiana* but with a twist, this version doesn't contain any Parmesan, and in true **MEZCLA** form, the sauce has gone in a very Mexican direction. I use the same salsa roja recipe as I do in the Chiles rellenos (page 166) – it's a great sauce to make ahead and have stashed in the fridge. These cheesy roasted aubergines are already very simple, and would be quicker to make still if the salsa was already taken care of. Serve with salad and grilled bread to mop up the sauce, or serve over pasta or polenta.

————

Preheat the oven to 230°C fan/250°C.

Cut deep cross-hatches into the flesh side of each aubergine half – cut nearly all the way down, taking care to not actually puncture the skin.

Lay the aubergines cut side up on a large baking tray, then rub oil and salt into each cut half – about 3 tablespoons of olive oil and ¾ teaspoon of fine salt (total) across the 6 halves. Bake for 35–40 minutes, rotating the tray halfway so they colour evenly. The aubergines should be soft all the way through and very well browned on top … I repeat, they should be very well browned on top! Please don't be afraid to brown your aubergines more than you think you should.

Meanwhile, make the salsa roja. Put the first 10 ingredients (everything except the water and tomato purée/paste) into a large sauté pan on a medium-high heat and fry for 15 minutes, stirring often, until the tomatoes have broken down and the onions are soft and golden-brown. Turn the heat down to medium or medium-low if the mixture starts to catch or burn at any point.

Discard the habanero (or squeeze it with the back of a spoon before removing it if you like heat, see *Notes*). Transfer the salsa to a blender with the water and tomato purée/paste and blend until completely smooth. Set aside.

Combine all the cheese mix ingredients in a medium bowl.

Once the aubergines have roasted and are well browned, remove the tray from the oven. Pour some salsa roja over each aubergine half, then spoon over the cheese mixture. Return to the oven (which should still be at 230°C fan/250°C) for 6–8 minutes, or until the cheese bubbles and turns golden-brown in parts.

Leave to cool for a few minutes, then drizzle with oil and serve.

sure.
finely ch,
chopped, and y
grated before you tu.

40g dried porcini

4 tablespoons olive oil, plus extra to serve

3 cloves of garlic, very finely chopped
    (not crushed!)

½ teaspoon chilli flakes
    (or less if you prefer)

10g fresh parsley (stalks and leaves),
    finely chopped, plus extra to serve

⅓ teaspoon fine salt

1½ tablespoons tomato purée/paste

about 50 twists of freshly ground
    black pepper

250g dried tagliatelle nests

40g Parmesan, very finely grated,
    plus extra to serve

3 tablespoons double cream

Vegan option

You can easily make this vegan by
using plant-based cheese and cream.

Notes

It's always good to have all your prep
done before you start cooking, but it's
especially important with this recipe,
as things happen rather quickly. Make
        ou have your porcini soaked and
            ed, garlic and parsley finely
                ur Parmesan finely
                    the heat on.

Porcini ragù

I'm not sure if you're allowed to call a sauce that doesn't contain meat, doesn't start with a soffritto, and that only cooks for 10 minutes a ragù, and yet because of the concentrated flavour of the dried porcini, this has all the intensity of a meat ragù that has simmered for hours. Anyone who has made the spicy mushroom lasagne from *Ottolenghi Flavour* will realise what I'm trying to achieve here: an abridged version of that ragù with the same intensity but without the hours chopping kilos of mushrooms (yes, I heard you!). This recipe is inspired by two of my favourite dishes at Ristorante Pizzeria Acone near where I grew up in Tuscany – *penne all'Aconese* and *tagliatelle alla Beppa*.

––––––––––

In a medium bowl, cover the porcini with boiling water and leave to soak for 10 minutes. Drain, reserving 75g of the soaking liquid. Very finely chop the porcini to mince consistency, then set aside.

Put the oil, garlic, chilli flakes, parsley and fine salt into a cold, large sauté pan on a medium-low heat. Very gently fry for 5 minutes until soft and lightly golden, turning the heat down if the garlic starts to brown.

Increase the heat to medium-high, then add the chopped porcini, tomato purée/paste and plenty of pepper. Stir-fry for 3 minutes, then set the pan aside while you boil the pasta.

Cook the pasta in salted boiling water for about 6 minutes, until al dente. Drain, reserving 350g of the pasta water.

Return the sauté pan with the porcini to a medium-high heat, then add the 350g of pasta water and the reserved 75g of porcini soaking liquid. Stir, and bring to a simmer. Once simmering, leave to bubble away for 3 minutes. Add half the Parmesan to the pan, stirring until it has melted before adding the rest. Lower the heat to medium, then stir in the cream, followed by the drained tagliatelle. Toss over the heat until the pasta and sauce have emulsified – about 1½ minutes.

Remove from the heat and serve at once, finished with as much olive oil and Parmesan as your heart desires.

Salad

1 large cucumber, peeled, halved
    and watery centre scraped out (260g)
5 ripe plum tomatoes (650g),
    chopped into 1½–2cm cubes,
    seeds discarded (360g)
⅓ teaspoon fine salt
½ large lime

Crumpet croutons

3 crumpets (160g), cut into 2½cm chunks
3 tablespoons olive oil
1 large clove of garlic,
    finely grated/crushed
¼ teaspoon fine salt
freshly ground black pepper

Chilli oil

4 tablespoons olive oil
1 large clove of garlic, very finely chopped
1½ teaspoons tomato purée/paste
1¼ teaspoons pul biber or Aleppo
    chilli flakes, plus extra to serve
¼ teaspoon Urfa chilli flakes,
    plus extra to serve
⅛ teaspoon fine salt

Tahini ginger sauce

60g tahini (shake the container
    well before using)
1 teaspoon peeled and finely grated
    fresh ginger
1½ tablespoons soy sauce
2 tablespoons lime juice
½ tablespoon water
1½ tablespoons maple syrup

Make ahead

The tahini ginger sauce will keep for up
to 3 days in the fridge. The chilli oil will
last for up to 3 weeks.

Tomato salad with tahini ginger sauce, chilli oil and crumpet croutons

I should really take the salad out of this title, because, let's be honest, we're all here for the crumpet croutons. Once baked, their inherent holes crisp up and allow for an extra crunchy crouton experience which will leave you wondering if you'll ever do it any other way again. Add these croutons to just about any salad in the book – they're especially wonderful atop a salad made from leftover curried roast chicken (page 222).

This salad uses Middle Eastern chillies in the oil, as well as many other ingredients that would never be used in Sichuan cuisine, but nonetheless it is very much inspired by the inimitable cucumber salad at Xi'an Biang Biang Noodles in East London (not the crumpet croutons part, of course).

————

Preheat the oven to 180°C fan/200°C.

For the salad, chop the cucumber into 1½–2cm cubes. Put them into a bowl with the tomatoes and fine salt and lightly crush with your hands. Set aside while you prepare the rest.

Put the crumpets on a flat baking tray with the oil, garlic, fine salt and plenty of pepper. Mix well and bake for about 14 minutes, tossing halfway, until crisp and golden-brown. Set aside to cool.

For the chilli oil, heat the olive oil in a small saucepan on a medium heat for 1½ minutes. Remove from the heat, add the garlic, tomato purée/paste, both chilli flakes and fine salt and whisk well to combine.

Put all the ingredients for the tahini ginger sauce into a medium bowl and whisk until smooth.

Add the tahini sauce and a third of the chilli oil to the bowl with the tomatoes and cucumbers. Stir together but don't overmix, you want the sauce to be streaky with the oil. Tip onto a lipped platter and squeeze over half a lime.

Sprinkle over some more pul biber and Urfa chilli. Finish with the remaining chilli oil and the croutons and serve.

Omelette

6 large eggs

120g full-fat coconut milk (at least 70%
    coconut extract) (see notes below)

½ teaspoon peeled and finely grated fresh
    ginger (or ¼ teaspoon ground ginger)

1 small clove of garlic, finely
    grated/crushed

1 teaspoon finely grated lime zest

¾ teaspoon fine salt

5g fresh chives, finely chopped

5g fresh coriander, finely chopped

40g spring greens, very thinly sliced
    (or use spinach/kale)

100g feta, broken into medium chunks

2 very ripe medium plantains
    (460g) (they should be nearly all
    black and quite soft, with only
    some yellow marks)

30g ghee (from a jar not a tin,
    see page 17) or unsalted butter

1 tablespoon olive oil, plus extra to serve

lime wedges, to serve

Scotch bonnet salsa

200g sweet, ripe cherry tomatoes,
    such as Datterini

1 lime: 1 teaspoon finely grated zest
    and 1 tablespoon juice

1½ tablespoons olive oil

¾ teaspoon flaked salt, plus extra to serve

1–2 Scotch bonnet chillies (or a milder
    chilli if you prefer)

Make ahead

The salsa will keep for up to a week in
the fridge.

Notes

You'll only use 120g of coconut milk, but
take all the contents out of the tin and
whisk well to combine the solid and the
liquid before measuring out what's needed.

Upside down plantain omelette with Scotch bonnet salsa

My mother, a Brazilian who grew up in Cuba, is obsessed with plantain. She eats them alongside pretty much every meal and brought my sister and me up in the same way, so now my fruit bowl is almost never without a couple of blackening plantains. There is a plantain recipe for every stage of ripeness, from hard and green to soft and black. This recipe calls for plantains that are ripe and sweet, preferably nearly *all* black, with only some canary yellow marks. In truth, I'll only ever cook plantain at this stage of ripeness. Unripe/green plantain is no substitute here because you won't get that sweet, caramelised layer we're looking for.

———

Preheat the oven to 180°C fan/200°C.

In a large bowl, whisk together the eggs, coconut milk (see notes), ginger, garlic, lime zest and ½ teaspoon of fine salt. Stir in the chives, coriander, spring greens and feta, then set aside.

Peel the plantains and slice into ¾cm-thick rounds. You need about 320g of peeled slices.

Place a 28cm ovenproof, non-stick frying pan on a medium-high heat and add the ghee and the oil. Once the ghee has melted, layer the plantain slices to cover the bottom of the pan, then set a timer for 3 minutes and cook without stirring or flipping the plantain, to create a caramelised, golden layer on the bottom of the pan. Lower the heat, then pour over the egg mixture to evenly cover the base, and leave to fry for another 1 minute undisturbed. The omelette should be set around the edges but still liquid in the middle.

Transfer the pan to the oven and bake for about 8–9 minutes, or until the omelette is just set on top, with a good wobble in the centre. Don't be afraid of this wobble – the omelette will set a little as it cools, but also we (or at least I) want the omelette to have a soft, oozing centre! Leave to cool for 5 minutes, then use a spatula to release the sides of the omelette from the pan.

While the omelette is in the oven, make the salsa. Finely chop the cherry tomatoes into very small pieces. Transfer to a medium bowl, using your hands as a natural sieve so you don't take all the liquid and seeds with you (otherwise the salsa will be quite soggy). Stir in the lime zest, lime juice, oil and flaked salt.

Continues on next page...

Plantain omelette continued...

Very finely chop the Scotch bonnet – they vary substantially in heat level, so start with a quarter of a chilli, removing the seeds and pith if you prefer a milder heat. Add to the salsa, stir and taste, then add more to taste, up to 2 finely chopped chillies.

Place a large plate on top of the pan, then quickly flip the whole thing over so the omelette ends up on the plate. Hopefully all the plantain pieces will end up on the omelette, but if not, just peel them from the pan and place them back on top, golden-brown side up.

Drizzle with a little oil and sprinkle with flaked salt. Serve with the salsa on the side, and some extra lime wedges squeezed on top.

Triple citrus tomato salad (or soup)

3–5 ripe beef or Merinda tomatoes
  (they'll vary in size, but you want
  about 650g)

½ lemon

½ lime

½ tangerine

1 teaspoon maple syrup

5 tablespoons olive oil

2 cloves of garlic, very thinly
  sliced on a mandolin

30g fresh ginger, peeled and julienned

1 red chilli, pith and seeds removed,
  then julienned

1 jalapeño, pith and seeds removed,
  then julienned

5g fresh chives, finely chopped

flaked salt

crème fraîche or yoghurt, to serve
  (if making soup)

grilled bread, to serve (optional)

This recipe harnesses the potential of lime, lemon and tangerine when used in combination to create a simple yet delicious dressing (see also Sausage and charred citrus traybake, page 118). The result can be one of two things – salad or soup – depending on whether you plate or blitz the ingredients. If your tomatoes are particularly ripe and wonderful it might seem like a crime to blitz them, but trust me that the chilled soup version of this dish is also pretty great. Serve the salad with grilled bread to mop up all the juices. The soup is lovely topped with crumpet croutons (page 29).

———————

Slice your tomatoes as thin as you can (or cut into random bite-size chunks if you prefer) and arrange on a lipped platter. If you're making soup, just put them into a large bowl. Sprinkle generously with 1 teaspoon of flaked salt, then squeeze over the lemon, lime and tangerine. Drizzle over the maple syrup, then set aside while you fry the aromatics.

Put the oil into a medium saucepan on a medium heat. Once hot, add the garlic, ginger, chillies and ½ teaspoon of flaked salt. Gently fry, stirring with a fork to separate the aromatics, until the garlic and ginger are crisp and a light golden-brown. This should take 4–5 minutes but keep a close eye on them as they turn from golden to brown and burned quite quickly.

If making salad, spoon some of the oil and all the aromatics over the tomatoes, then let the tomatoes rest in the juices for at least 5 minutes (preferably 10 minutes) before finishing with the chives.

If making soup, hold back half the crispy aromatics and all the chives to top with, then put everything else into a blender and blitz until completely smooth. Serve chilled or warm with a spoonful of crème fraîche, a drizzle of oil, and the reserved crispy aromatics and chives sprinkled on top.

1 medium Napa cabbage (800g)

1½ teaspoons flaked salt

2 tablespoons olive oil, plus extra to serve

1 crunchy apple or pear

5g fresh basil leaves

3 spring onions, julienned (30g)

pecorino or Parmesan shavings
    to serve (optional)

Dressing

1 tablespoon lemon juice

1 tablespoon lime juice

1 teaspoon tomato purée/paste

1 teaspoon maple syrup or honey

1 teaspoon red bell pepper flakes

¼ small clove of garlic, finely
    grated/crushed

2 tablespoons olive oil, plus extra to serve

100g sweet, ripe cherry tomatoes, such
    as Datterini, very finely chopped

Roasted and raw cabbage with tomato, lemon and lime dressing

This salad showcases Napa cabbage (my favourite cabbage but you could use any cabbage, really) in raw and roasted form, meaning that you get a lovely combination of fresh crunch and soft, sweet char in every bite.

The dressing doubles up as a salsa, and works really well alongside steak, grilled fish or roast chicken.

————

Preheat the oven to 220°C fan/240°C.

Cut the base off the cabbage, then separate the cabbage leaves. Cut any of the larger leaves in half lengthways down the centre of the rib. Place the cabbage in a large bowl with the flaked salt. Massage the salt into the leaves for 1 minute, until they are beginning to soften.

Transfer just over half of the leaves to a large, flat, parchment-lined baking tray with the oil and toss to combine. Roast for 10-12 minutes, tossing halfway, until the edges are nicely browned and beginning to crisp up. Set aside while you prepare the rest.

In a small bowl, whisk all the ingredients for the dressing together until the tomato purée/paste is incorporated.

Cut the apple or pear into thick matchsticks and mix together with the raw cabbage. Pile about a quarter of the raw cabbage mixture on a large plate, followed by a quarter of the dressing, a quarter of the roasted cabbage leaves and a quarter of the basil and spring onion. Continue in the same way, piling the veg up on top of each other until you've used it all up.

Top with pecorino or Parmesan shavings (optional), then finish with a good drizzle of oil and serve.

2 large ripe mangoes (not too hard,
    not too soft, see intro) – peaches
    would be lovely too
100g hard Cheddar-style goats'
    cheese (or use mature Cheddar
    or young pecorino)
green ends of 4 spring onions, thinly
    sliced into rounds
2 jalapeños, thinly sliced into rounds
flaked salt
extra virgin olive oil, to serve

Quick pickled shallots
1 banana shallot (30g), thinly sliced
    into rounds
2 tablespoons lemon juice
¼ teaspoon fine salt

Dressing
4 tablespoons olive oil
½ teaspoon fine salt
2½ tablespoons lime juice
1 tablespoon maple syrup
½ teaspoon toasted sesame oil

Mango and cheese salad with jalapeño and lime

I love the combination of fruit and cheese. This salad, for want of a better descriptor, can work in any context: as a starter, as part of a spread or as a cheese course. You could even pile all the components onto grilled bread and call it a *crostino*. You'll need a ripe mango for this (peaches or golden plums would be lovely too), but it shouldn't be so soft that you can't peel and slice it into chunks.

————

Put all the ingredients for the pickled shallots into a small bowl and mix to combine. Leave for 10 minutes to 1 hour (but no longer, or they'll be too soft).

For the dressing, mix the oil, salt, lime juice, maple syrup and sesame oil together, just to combine. Don't overmix or it will begin to thicken – the dressing should be light and thin.

Peel the mangoes and cut the flesh into random chunks or slices. Cut the cheese into random slices.

Arrange the mango and cheese on a platter and spoon over some of the dressing (you won't need it all). Top with the spring onions, jalapeños and pickled shallots. Finish with some extra virgin olive oil and flaked salt, and serve.

Notes
Try swapping the cheese for raw or cured fish. Everything else stays the same, just change the name of the dish to 'Mango and fish crudo with jalapeño and lime'.

2 tablespoons olive oil

2 tablespoons ghee (from a jar not
   a tin, see page 17) or unsalted butter

1 red Scotch bonnet, halved (or a
   milder chilli if you prefer)

3 large, ripe plantains (700g) (they
   should be nearly all black and quite
   soft, with only some yellow marks),
   peeled, halved widthways and cut
   into bite-size pieces

½ teaspoon garam masala

½ tablespoon maple syrup

flaked salt

1 lime, cut into wedges, to serve

Plantains with Scotch bonnet, garam masala and lime

You'll need soft, ripe plantains for this recipe – they should be nearly all black, with only some yellow markings. Serve as a side to savoury dishes like roast chicken, grilled fish or fried tofu.

———————

Put the oil, ghee and Scotch bonnet into a large sauté pan on a medium-high heat and gently cook until the ghee has melted.

Add the plantain and spread out as much as possible. Sprinkle with ½ teaspoon of flaked salt, then gently fry (don't stir!) for 2½ minutes, or until the bottoms are golden-brown.

Toss the plantain, then continue to gently fry for another 2½ minutes until the other sides are golden-brown (again, don't stir, just let them colour).

Lower the heat all the way down. Add the garam masala and maple syrup, cover with a lid and continue to cook for another 2½ minutes, until soft and cooked through.

Transfer to a platter, squeeze over the lime wedges and serve.

Notes

Don't let these plantains sit around once they've been fried; you want to eat them straight out of the pan when they are soft and hot, as they harden while they sit.

Spicy ginger, tomato and sesame dip

6 tablespoons mild olive oil

2 teaspoons toasted sesame oil

1½ tablespoons sesame seeds

20g ginger, peeled and very
    finely chopped

5 cloves of garlic, very finely
    chopped (15g)

½ onion, very finely chopped (80g)

130g sweet, ripe cherry tomatoes, such
    as Datterini, very finely chopped

1½ tablespoons tomato purée/paste

1 tablespoon red bell pepper flakes
    (or use ½ tablespoon pul biber
    or Aleppo chilli)

2 teaspoons caster sugar/maple syrup

¾ teaspoon fine salt

1 teaspoon soy sauce

2 teaspoons lime juice

2 tablespoons tahini, to serve (optional)

I call this a dip but it could be anything you want it to be: dip, sauce, condiment and everything in between.

Make sure you chop the ginger, garlic, onion and tomatoes as finely as possible, so they really soften as they cook. Serve as a dip for crunchy veg/crisps/hunks of cheese, or as a sauce for noodles, or as a condiment with anything from dumplings to roast pork to grilled fish.

————————

Put the first 12 ingredients (everything except the lime juice and tahini) into a large sauté pan and place on a very low heat. Gently cook for 30 minutes, stirring often, or until everything is soft and very fragrant. This is a slow process, so be sure to keep the heat very low throughout – you don't want any of the elements to fry and become crispy.

Remove from the heat and stir in the lime juice. If serving as a dip, leave to cool for 5 minutes before transferring to a platter and drizzling over some tahini. Alternatively, serve as a condiment for noodles, dumplings etc. (see intro).

Make ahead

The dip will last for up to 3 days in the fridge.

Notes

If you have a food processor, simply add the first 12 ingredients and pulse until everything is very finely chopped, rather than chopping everything individually by hand.

An image of this recipe is on page 44.

Ricotta dip with hot sauce butter pine nuts

Hot sauce butter pine nuts

20g pine nuts

40g ghee (from a jar not a tin, see
    page 17) or unsalted butter

1 tablespoon olive oil

1 clove of garlic, finely grated/crushed

2 tablespoons hot sauce (I use Kold
    Sauce but you could use Encona
    or Tabasco)

¾ teaspoon smoked paprika

⅛ teaspoon fine salt (you may need
    more depending on how salty
    your hot sauce is)

Ricotta dip

½ cucumber, peeled, halved and
    watery centre scraped out

150g full-fat ricotta

100g Greek-style yoghurt

1½ teaspoons finely grated lemon zest
    (reserve the rest of the lemon to serve)

½ small clove of garlic,
    finely grated/crushed

¼ teaspoon fine salt

freshly ground black pepper

10g fresh chives, finely chopped

3 spring onions, finely sliced

Yes, this is a dip but it's also so much more than a dip. It can be scooped up with anything from crisps to crunchy veg to chicken wings, it can be stirred through cooled pasta or potatoes to make pasta salad or potato salad respectively, or it can be a base on which to serve grilled lamb chops, barbecued chicken, schnitzels or asparagus (both blanched and grilled work really well). These are just a few of many options for this combination of flavours – let your imagination run wild.

————

For the hot sauce butter pine nuts, put the pine nuts into a medium frying pan on a medium-high heat and cook, tossing the nuts every now and then, until nicely browned all over, 3–4 minutes. Remove from the heat and add all the remaining ingredients. Stir together and set aside to infuse for 5 minutes. If you leave it for too long it will set a bit, in which case just gently melt before serving so it's liquid again.

For the dip, cut the cucumber into 1cm cubes. Mix the cucumber with the ricotta, yoghurt, lemon zest, garlic, salt and plenty of pepper. Stir in half each of the chives and spring onions.

Spoon the dip on to a plate and top with the hot sauce butter pine nuts. Finish with the remaining chives and spring onions. Serve with the lemon wedges.

Notes

Use grated tomato instead of hot sauce
for a chilli-free version.

An image of this recipe is on page 45.

2 baby gem lettuces, washed
    and leaves separated
10g mixed fresh herbs (I like to use
    a mix of coriander, mint and basil)
2 green chillies, thinly sliced into
    rounds (optional)
20g spring onion green ends,
    thinly sliced into rounds
2 teaspoons mixed black and
    white sesame seeds, well
    toasted, lightly crushed and
    tossed with some flaked salt
lime wedges, for serving

Quick pickled shallots

1 shallot, thinly sliced into rounds
2 tablespoons lemon juice
½ teaspoon caster sugar
¼ teaspoon fine salt

Dressing

60g olive oil
½ teaspoon fine salt
40g lime juice
20g maple syrup
½ teaspoon toasted sesame oil
5g fresh chives, finely chopped

Gem and herb salad with maple, lime and sesame dressing

The star of the show is the dressing, which is sweet from the maple syrup, sour from the lime juice and nutty from the toasted sesame oil. Feel free to experiment with the herbs you include, as well as the salad leaves. I've suggested baby gem, but bitter leaves such as chicory or radicchio would also work well, as would endive, butter lettuce or frisée. You could also add slices of fennel or cucumber to up the crunch factor.

———————

Put all the ingredients for the pickled shallots into a small bowl and mix to combine. Pickle for 15 minutes to 1 hour (but no longer, or they'll become too soft).

For the dressing, mix the oil, salt, lime juice, maple syrup and sesame oil together just to combine. Don't overmix or it will emulsify and thicken – the dressing should be light and thin.

When ready to plate, stir the chives into the dressing. Put the lettuce and herbs into a large bowl and pour over the dressing. Add the pickled shallots, chillies and spring onions and toss together. Finish with the sesame seeds and serve with extra lime wedges for squeezing over.

Notes

This image also shows Limey cucumber salad with charred spring onion salsa, see page 64.

Dumplings

200g frozen spinach, defrosted
(frozen weight)

15g fresh basil

10g fresh chives, roughly chopped

2 cloves of garlic, finely grated/crushed

1 teaspoon finely grated lemon zest

¼ teaspoon freshly grated nutmeg

30g white miso paste

40g olive oil, plus extra for greasing

⅓ teaspoon fine salt

about 30 twists of freshly ground
black pepper

200g plant-based or regular milk

60g fine, quick-cook polenta (see intro)

Cherry tomato sauce

3 tablespoons olive oil, plus extra to serve

20g dairy-free (or regular) unsalted butter

3 cloves of garlic, very finely chopped

280g sweet, ripe cherry tomatoes, such
as Datterini, roughly chopped

⅓ teaspoon fine salt

¼ teaspoon chilli flakes (optional)

5 fresh sage leaves

5g fresh basil leaves, plus extra to serve

about 10 twists of freshly ground
black pepper

3 tablespoons water

Make ahead

The spinach and herb paste will keep for
up to 3 days in the fridge.

Notes

If you don't need these to be vegan, you
can add Parmesan to the dumpling mix
(in which case you won't need as much
salt). I haven't experimented with a vegan
Parmesan alternative, but I'm sure that
would work too.

Spinach and herb dumplings with cherry tomato sauce

These are inspired by *malfatti* (spinach, ricotta and semolina dumplings), but because I wanted them to be vegan, they don't contain the ricotta, Parmesan and egg that are synonymous with malfatti. While I was making these dumplings vegan, I thought, what the hell, why not make them gluten-free too, so I experimented and finally landed on using polenta as a binder in place of semolina and egg. Their lack of dairy and egg make these dumplings less rich and creamy than malfatti, but that's not to say they're not delicious in their own right.

Make sure you use fine, quick-cook polenta (aka instant polenta) here, rather than the coarse variety. Check the side of the packet and as long as the cook time is 8 minutes or less, you're good to go.

———————

Squeeze the defrosted spinach to get rid of any water – you should end up with 100g squeezed spinach. Put the spinach, herbs, garlic, lemon zest, nutmeg, miso, oil, fine salt and pepper into a blender or small food processor and blitz to a smooth paste, scraping down the sides as needed.

In a medium saucepan on a medium heat, warm up the milk until steaming. Turn the heat to low, add the polenta and whisk continuously for about 2½ minutes, or until you get a very thick paste that's coming away from the sides and bottom of the pan. Remove from the heat. Add the green paste and stir vigorously until it's completely incorporated. Leave to cool for 2–3 minutes.

Oil your hands and shape the mixture into 12 balls weighing about 30g each. Transfer them to a large bowl/container and cover with a lid or plate, to keep them warm.

For the sauce, put all the ingredients except the water into a large sauté pan on a medium-high heat. Fry for 5 minutes, stirring often, then lower the heat to medium and cook for another 2 minutes, stirring, until the tomatoes have softened and broken down. Stir in the water.

Place the dumplings in the sauce and cover with a lid. Turn the heat down to low and cook for 3 minutes. Top with fresh basil, a good drizzle of olive oil and some flaked salt. Serve at once (the dumplings will harden as they cool).

Kohlrabi with miso meunière

3 large kohlrabi, stalks removed
and peeled (1.1kg)

3 tablespoons olive oil

1½ teaspoons fine salt

1 lemon, cut into wedges, to serve

Miso meuniere

150g unsalted butter, cut into
cubes (use a plant-based
butter to make this vegan)

2 cloves of garlic, very finely chopped
(not crushed!)

⅛ teaspoon fine salt

20g white miso paste

2 tablespoons lemon juice

30g baby (nonpareille) capers (or
normal capers, roughly chopped)

5g fresh parsley, very finely chopped

10g fresh chives, very finely chopped

This is inspired by the recipe for Celeriac steaks with Cafe de Paris sauce in *Ottolenghi Flavour*, a dish that proves that vegetables can be just as exciting a centrepiece as meat or fish. This meunière sauce deviates from tradition by containing miso, garlic and chives and whilst it's very special with kohlrabi, it would also go really well with grilled asparagus, mashed potatoes, scallops, fish, steak, roast chicken ... or just about anything savoury. If you can't get hold of kohlrabi, serve the sauce with celeriac steaks (see page 69 of *Ottolenghi Flavour*, if you have a copy).

————————

Preheat the oven to 180°C fan/200°C.

Use a sharp knife to shave off the dry top and bottom of each peeled kohlrabi bulb, then cut each bulb widthways into 2cm-thick steaks. You should have about 9 steaks.

In a large bowl, mix the steaks together with the oil and salt, then arrange on a large, flat baking tray, spaced apart (you may need to spread across two trays if your tray isn't big enough). Roast for 50–55 minutes, or until the kohlrabi steaks are soft and cooked through, and the undersides are nicely browned. Turn the oven off and keep the steaks warm in the oven while you make the sauce (this will also help them soften further).

When the steaks have finished roasting, make the sauce. Place the butter in a medium, non-stick frying pan and place on a medium-low heat. Gently cook for about 4 minutes, swirling the pan while the butter melts, begins to foam, then turns a light golden colour. Lower the heat all the way down, add the garlic and salt and continue to cook for 1½ minutes, swirling the pan. Add the miso and lemon juice and cook for another 1 minute, whisking the miso into the sauce. Remove from the heat, then stir in the capers and herbs.

Serve the kohlrabi steaks browned sides up with the sauce spooned on top, and lemon wedges on the side.

Notes

Kohlrabi is not as tough to cut into as, say, pumpkin, but nonetheless, take care when slicing them into steaks; you'll need to use a large, sharp knife.

400g oyster mushrooms

6 x 22cm metal or wooden skewers
    (see notes below)

Chilli oil

80g olive oil

60g rose harissa (or 30g regular
    harissa, plus 2 tablespoons olive oil)

¾ teaspoon Urfa chilli flakes

¾ teaspoon caster sugar

¼ teaspoon fine salt

Crushed chickpeas

300g jarred chickpeas (drained weight)

1 small clove of garlic, finely
    grated/crushed

80g Greek-style yoghurt, plus 20g
    to serve (use coconut yoghurt
    to keep this vegan)

1 tablespoon olive oil

Salsa verde

5g fresh coriander, finely chopped

10g fresh chives, finely chopped

2 tablespoons olive oil

2 tablespoons lime juice

flaked salt

Make ahead

The chilli oil will keep in the fridge for
up to 3 weeks.

Notes

Soak wooden skewers in water for
20 minutes before use, so they don't burn.

I use jarred chickpeas here as they are
soft and perfectly seasoned. You can
use tinned or home-cooked chickpeas,
but you'll need to adjust the seasoning.

Crispy oyster mushroom skewers
with crushed chickpeas

There is a hierarchy of mushrooms, in my opinion, and oyster mushrooms are right at the very top, along with porcini. If you're not already familiar with the wonders of pan-fried or roasted oyster mushrooms, you're in for a treat, because this unassuming mushroom transforms into a crispy, succulent version of itself when high heat is applied. These skewers aren't meant to look or taste like meat, and yet ...

Preheat the oven to 220°C fan/240°C.

For the chilli oil, mix all the ingredients together in a large bowl.

Tear any larger mushrooms in half and keep the small ones whole. Put them into the bowl with the chilli oil. Mix well – the mushrooms should be completely coated with the oil.

Line a flat baking tray with parchment paper. Thread the mushrooms on to the skewers and arrange them on the tray, spaced apart. Roast for about 18 minutes, basting halfway, until the edges of the mushrooms are crisp and golden-brown.

While the mushrooms are roasting, put all the ingredients for the crushed chickpeas into a large bowl and roughly crush with a potato masher (or pulse in a food processor). Add salt to taste – you'll need more if your chickpeas weren't salted to start with. I like the contrast between room-temperature chickpeas and hot mushrooms, but you can warm up the chickpeas if you prefer.

When you're ready to serve, mix all the ingredients for the salsa together with a good pinch of flaked salt.

Spread the chickpeas on a platter, then swirl through the remaining 20g of yoghurt. Top with the skewers and the chilli oil from the tray. Spoon over the salsa verde and serve.

1 loaf of sourdough or focaccia

300g mature Cheddar cheese,
    roughly grated

150g double cream

50g Greek yoghurt

1 jalapeño or green chilli, very
    thinly sliced (optional)

½ onion, very thinly sliced
    on a mandolin

flaked salt

*Spring onion, honey
and Urfa butter*

50g unsalted butter, cut into
    smaller pieces

2 tablespoons olive oil

3 large cloves of garlic, very
    finely chopped

2–3 spring onions, green ends very
    thinly sliced into rounds (20g)

25g manuka honey (or another
    floral honey)

¾ teaspoon Urfa chilli flakes

¼ teaspoon fine salt

Giant cheese on toast with spring onion, honey and Urfa butter

This is basically a giant, fancy cheese on toast using the bottom half of a loaf of sourdough (focaccia would also work really well). Cut it up into smaller squares and serve as a sharing snack, or cut into quarters and serve with a fried egg and a zingy salad for lunch or dinner. I like to use manuka honey in the butter because of its beautifully floral flavour, but you absolutely don't have to use anything that fancy.

By all means, use both halves of the loaf and double the toppings and butter if you're feeding a crowd.

———————

Preheat the oven to 230°C fan/250°C.

Halve the loaf of bread widthways (you only want the bottom half for this recipe) and place the bottom half on a flat baking tray, cut side up. Once the oven is hot, bake for 4–5 minutes, or until the surface is golden and lightly toasted.

In a medium bowl, mix together the cheese, cream and yoghurt. Remove the bread from the oven and spread the cheese mixture all over it (don't flatten the surface, you want cheesy hills). Return to the top shelf of the oven and bake for 8–9 minutes, or until the surface is browned and bubbling. Turn to the highest grill setting to melt/brown further if necessary.

While the bread is in the oven, put all the ingredients for the butter into a medium saucepan on a medium-low heat and cook for 4 minutes. You want the garlic to soften but not to brown or become crispy, so turn the heat down if needed.

Spoon the butter over the cheesy bread, then finish with the jalapeño and onion. If you have a blowtorch, use it to char the onions slightly. Sprinkle with flaked salt and serve.

Notes

I've used a fair amount of honey because
I love the combination of sweet and
savoury. If you're less keen, add less honey.

Garlic yoghurt with crispy herbs

200g Greek yoghurt

80g mascarpone

1 small clove of garlic, finely
    grated/crushed

1 lemon: 1 teaspoon finely grated
    zest and ½ tablespoon juice

about 5 twists of freshly ground
    black pepper

20g fresh dill leaves, patted dry

10g fresh coriander leaves, patted dry

10g fresh basil leaves, patted dry

3½ tablespoons olive oil

¼ teaspoon pul biber or Aleppo
    chilli flakes (optional)

¼ teaspoon Urfa chilli flakes (optional)

1 teaspoon black sesame seeds, toasted

flaked sea salt

grilled bread, crisps or crunchy
    veg, to serve

Crispy herbs are a lovely thing, and I've found that you can get a whole lot done more easily, and with much less oil, if you crisp them up in a hot oven. Make sure your herbs are fresh and green; older, wilting herbs that are beginning to brown won't work here, as the heat of the oven will just accelerate their demise. Use soft herbs like dill, basil, coriander and parsley, rather than hard herbs like sage and rosemary, which will become extremely bitter in the oven.

Try these crispy herbs on top of salads, pasta dishes and raw fish dishes, as well as with this dip.

———————

Preheat the oven to 220°C fan/240°C.

Put the yoghurt, mascarpone, garlic, lemon zest, black pepper and ½ teaspoon of fine salt into a medium bowl and whip for 1–2 minutes until thickened to the consistency of soft-serve ice cream.

On a flat baking tray, mix all the herbs together with 1½ tablespoons of oil, then spread them out on the tray as much as possible. Bake for 2½–3½ minutes, checking after 2½ minutes, until the herbs are crisp but still bright green. Transfer the herbs to a plate to cool for a few minutes and sprinkle generously with flaked salt.

Spoon the yoghurt on to a large plate and create a well in the centre with the back of the spoon. Fill the well with the remaining 2 tablespoons of oil and ½ tablespoon of lemon juice.

Arrange the herbs around the edges of the yoghurt, then sprinkle with the pul biber and Urfa chilli, if using, and black sesame seeds. Serve with grilled bread, crisps or crunchy veg.

Make ahead

The yoghurt will keep for up to 3 days in the fridge.

Notes

The garlic yoghurt is lovely with slow-roasted garlic instead of raw garlic. If you have the time, preheat the oven to 220°C fan/240°C, cut the top off a whole garlic bulb to expose the cloves, then wrap the bulb in foil and roast for 40 minutes. Squeeze the cooked garlic out of its papery skin, finely chop, then add to the yoghurt.

1 medium Savoy cabbage

1 teaspoon flaked salt

3 tablespoons olive oil

1 jalapeño, thinly sliced into
    rounds (optional)

5g fresh herbs (preferably
    a mix of dill and coriander)

Greek-style yoghurt, to serve (optional)

lemon wedges, to serve

Mango and harissa salsa

3 tablespoons olive oil

4 large cloves of garlic,
    very finely chopped

1 mild red chilli, deseeded and
    very finely chopped

⅛ teaspoon fine salt

2 tablespoons rose harissa

2 teaspoons tomato purée/paste

100g very ripe, sweet mango
    flesh, peeled and chopped
    into 1cm cubes

2 teaspoons lemon juice

Roasted cabbage with mango and harissa salsa

The mango and harissa salsa is the star here and couldn't be easier to put together. It works well in so many contexts: try it with roast chicken, marinated tofu or grilled fish or prawns, or let it come to room temperature and use it as the base for a fish or prawn crudo dish. For a quick midweek dinner, serve the cabbage with fried eggs.

———————

Preheat the oven to 220°C fan/240°C.

Separate the cabbage leaves to get 400g of the brightest green leaves (save the rest for another recipe). Cut the leaves in half along the ribs, then cut in half again. Put them into a large bowl with the flaked salt and oil and massage together. Transfer to a large, flat tray and spread out as much as possible – it's fine if some leaves overlap, as they'll shrink. Roast for 12 minutes, tossing the leaves halfway, until the edges are beginning to brown and crisp up.

To make the salsa, put the oil, garlic, chilli and fine salt into a large sauté pan and place on a medium-low heat. Gently fry for 6–7 minutes, stirring often, until the garlic is very soft. You don't want the garlic to brown, so turn the heat down if necessary. Remove the pan from the heat. Stir in the harissa and tomato purée/paste until combined, then stir in the mango and lemon juice.

Spoon the salsa on to a platter and top with the roasted cabbage leaves. Squeeze over some lemon juice, then top with the jalapeño and herbs. Serve warm with yoghurt on the side, if you like.

Get ahead

The mango and harissa salsa will keep in the fridge for up to 3 days, after which the mango might start to get a little fizzy and funky (which actually tastes quite nice).

Pickled red onions

½ red onion, thinly sliced
    on a mandolin
3 tablespoons lemon juice
⅛ teaspoon fine salt

Turmeric fried onions

4 tablespoons olive oil
2 medium onions, very finely
    chopped (280g)
¾ teaspoon fine salt
2 tablespoons maple syrup
    or runny honey
1½ teaspoons ground turmeric

Roasted spring onions

3–4 small bunches of thin spring
    onions (350g)
3 tablespoons olive oil
½ teaspoon fine salt

Roasted, pickled and fried onions (aka onion party)

Featuring sweet turmeric fried onions, charred spring onions and sour pickled onions, this vibrant dish is just as much of a party for the eyes as it is for the mouth. Serve it as a side to roast chicken, pork or grilled fish, or pile the whole lot on top of some labne or the Garlic yoghurt on page 59 and serve as a dip with crusty grilled bread.

———

Preheat the oven to 230°C fan/250°C.

Put all the ingredients for the pickled red onions into a medium bowl, mix together and set aside.

For the turmeric fried onions, place the oil, onions and salt in a medium, non-stick frying pan on a medium-low heat. Gently fry for 20–22 minutes, or until soft and golden-brown. This is a slow caramelisation process so don't be tempted to turn the heat up to speed things up. Remove from the heat and stir in the maple syrup and turmeric.

Trim the tops and bottoms of the spring onions; you want them to be about 23cm long. If your spring onions are thin, keep them whole. If they are particularly thick, halve them lengthways.

Place on a large, flat tray with the oil and salt, mix well then spread out. Roast for 8 minutes, or until softened and slightly charred.

Spoon the fried onions on to a platter and top with the roasted spring onions. Finish with the pickled onions along with most of the pickling liquid and serve.

Serves 4

2 medium cucumbers, peeled,
    halved and watery centres
    scraped out (400g)
2–4 limes, juiced to get 60g
½ tablespoon flaked salt
1 baby gem lettuce, leaves separated (60g)

Charred spring onion salsa

7 spring onions (95g)
20g fresh chives, finely chopped
½ jalapeño or green chilli,
    finely chopped (optional)
4 tablespoons olive oil
¼ teaspoon fine salt

Limey cucumber salad with charred spring onion salsa

This is one of those zingy salads that will go with just about anything, though the charred spring onion salsa and the lime-pickled cucumbers make it that much more exciting than your average bowl of mixed leaves. Once you've followed the recipe a couple of times you should feel confident to wing it and make it your own. Switch up the cucumber with celery, kohlrabi or fennel (or indeed, do a mix of some/all of them), or use whatever herbs you have in the fridge in place of the chives in the salsa. The charred spring onion salsa will keep for up to 2 days in the fridge, and it's a lovely condiment in its own right, so well worth doubling up on.

———————

Cut the cucumbers diagonally into 1½cm-thick slices. Put them into a bowl with the lime juice and flaked salt and toss together to coat. Set aside to pickle while you make the salsa, or for up to 1 hour.

For the salsa, heat a large frying pan on a high heat. Once very hot, place the spring onions in the pan and cook for 2–3 minutes on each side, or until nicely charred on both sides. Set aside to cool, then finely chop.

In a medium bowl, mix the chives and jalapeño with the oil and salt (you can also blitz these to make a lovely green oil, if you have a small enough processor). Add the chopped charred spring onions to the bowl and mix well.

When you're ready to serve, drain the cucumber through a sieve set over a large bowl to collect the salty lime juice. Reserve 25g of said juice, saving the rest to use in another dressing (or in a margarita!).

Transfer the drained cucumber to the bowl with the charred spring onion salsa and mix well.

Place the lettuce in a large bowl with the 25g of salty lime juice and toss, then add the cucumbers and toss again. Serve at once.

Notes

This salad gets soggy quite quickly, so mix it all together just before serving.

An image of this recipe is on page 47.

80g dendê marinade (page 89)

1 very ripe plantain (mostly black,
    with only some yellow marks)

50g mayonnaise (preferably Kewpie,
    but any will do)

1 tablespoon lime juice

Creamed plantain with dendê, ginger and lime

This creamed plantain is flavoured with dendê (page 15), ginger, lime and chilli and goes very well with roast pork or chicken, grilled fish, and the prawns on page 89. It's sweet, sour and quite punchy, which makes it great as both a condiment and a side dish.

————————

First make the dendê marinade. Make half the recipe on page 89, or make a full batch and keep the leftovers in the fridge for up to a week.

Leaving the skin on, cut the ends off the plantain, then cut it into thirds widthways. Place in a medium saucepan and cover with boiling water. Cook on a medium heat until the plantain is very soft, about 20 minutes. Remove the skin and while still hot, transfer the flesh to a food processor with the dendê marinade, mayo and lime. Blitz until completely smooth, then serve warm.

Notes

An image of this recipe is on page 88.

Buttery porcini fried eggs

30g dried porcini

30g unsalted butter

3 tablespoons olive oil

2 large cloves of garlic, very finely chopped

1 tablespoon fresh parsley, finely chopped,
    plus a few sprigs to serve

1 tablespoon fresh chives, finely chopped

about 10 twists of black pepper

¼ teaspoon fine salt

4 large eggs

1 lemon

freshly grated Parmesan, to serve

chipotle or regular chilli flakes,
    to serve (optional)

Unsurprisingly these eggs are perfect for breakfast, but as porcini mushrooms are so meaty, they also work really well as a light lunch or dinner. Serve with a green salad and bread to mop up all the garlic butter.

———

Cover the porcini with boiling water and leave to soak for 20 minutes. Drain the porcini, rinse them well, then pat them dry.

Put the butter, oil, garlic, herbs, black pepper and fine salt into a medium, non-stick frying pan on a medium heat. Once the butter has melted, add the porcini and fry for 2 minutes, stirring often.

Crack the eggs into the pan, lower the heat and cover with a lid. Cook until the whites are set and the yolks are still runny, 2½–4 minutes.

Use a small spoon to peel back the layer of white over the yolks to reveal them, if you like, then sprinkle the eggs with a bit of salt. Top with some finely grated lemon zest, a good squeeze of lemon juice and some grated Parmesan, then finish with parsley sprigs and chilli flakes (if using) and serve from the pan.

Cheesy polenta with curried onions

50g unsalted butter

3 tablespoons olive oil, plus extra to serve

3 onions, finely chopped (450g)

1⅛ teaspoons fine salt

1 habanero (optional)

1½ teaspoons medium curry powder

Polenta

400g whole milk

400g chicken stock (or veg stock/water)

1 clove of garlic, finely grated/crushed

1 teaspoon medium curry powder

1⅛ teaspoons fine salt

120g fine quick-cook polenta

100g Gruyère cheese, finely grated

15g unsalted butter

2 teaspoons white miso paste

The combination of cheese and curry might sound off-putting, but trust me, it works. The curried onions are one of my favourite condiments in the book and can be used in lots of different contexts (see Scallops with curried onions and lime, page 197). Try the onions swirled through labne or yoghurt and served as a dip, spooned on top of soured-cream-stuffed baked potatoes, over eggs, or in sandwiches, burgers or hot dogs. Serve this polenta with sausages, grilled meats or fish, or as part of a vegetarian spread.

—————

First make the onions. Put the butter, oil, onions, fine salt and habanero (if using) into a large sauté pan on a medium heat and cook, stirring often, for 18 minutes, until soft and golden. Reduce the heat to low and cook for another 4 minutes, stirring often, until deeply golden-brown. You want the onions to very slowly caramelise – don't be tempted to turn up the heat to speed up the process, and if they begin to catch or burn at any point, turn the heat down. Discard the habanero, stir in the curry powder and transfer to a bowl.

For the polenta, add the milk, stock or water, garlic, curry powder and salt to the same sauté pan and place on a medium heat. Once steaming, lower the heat all the way down and pour in the polenta slowly. Whisk continuously for about 7 minutes, or until the mixture has thickened and is completely smooth. Remove from the heat and stir in the cheese, butter and miso until combined.

Serve the polenta at once, as it will begin to harden straight away. Transfer to a platter or serve from the pan. Stir the onions through the surface and drizzle with olive oil.

Make ahead

The curried onions will last for up to a week in the fridge.

Notes

This image also shows Peas with tomatoes and onions, see page 70.

Peas with tomatoes and onions

1 onion, very finely chopped

6 tablespoons olive oil, plus extra to serve

1½ teaspoons fine salt

200g sweet, ripe cherry tomatoes,
    such as Datterini, halved

1½ teaspoons tomato purée/paste

4 large cloves of garlic, crushed
    with the side of a knife

15g fresh basil leaves

500g frozen garden peas, defrosted

150g chicken stock (or veg stock/water)

5g fresh chives, finely chopped

½ lemon

flaked salt, to serve

Soft, slow-cooked peas with tomatoes, garlic and plenty of oil is a humble combination you'll come across in various parts of Italy. There's not a whole lot going on here, which, in terms of this book, is quite rare. You could say that this dish 'does what it says on the tin', more or less, but that's not to say it's not completely delicious in its simplicity. I like to serve these peas at room temperature, with warm bread to mop up all the tomatoey, garlicky, oily broth. Serve with burrata, soft-boiled eggs or shaved pecorino, if you don't need this to be vegan.

———————

Put the onion, 2 tablespoons of olive oil and ½ teaspoon of fine salt into a large sauté pan on a medium heat and gently fry for 8 minutes, stirring often. Lower the heat all the way down and continue to fry for 2 minutes, or until the onion is soft and very deeply golden, stirring often.

Add the remaining 4 tablespoons of oil to the pan along with the tomatoes, tomato purée/paste, garlic, 10g of the basil and the remaining 1 teaspoon of fine salt. Increase the heat to medium and cook for 4 minutes, stirring every now and then, until the tomatoes are beginning to soften.

Stir in the peas and stock or water, bring to a simmer, then cook for 6 minutes until the liquid has reduced a little (it should still be quite saucy, though).

Remove from the heat. Leave to cool for 10 minutes (I like these peas warm not hot), then stir in the chives and juice from the lemon. Top with the remaining basil, finish with some oil and flaked salt and serve.

Notes

An image of this recipe is on page 69.

Pineapple pizza salsa

70g olive oil

50g tomato purée/paste

¾ teaspoon smoked paprika

1 large clove of garlic, finely chopped
    (not crushed)

1 teaspoon red bell pepper flakes

½ teaspoon chilli flakes (or ¼ teaspoon
    if you prefer milder heat)

½ teaspoon dried oregano

up to 2 teaspoons caster sugar
    (start with less if your pineapple
    is particularly sweet)

⅓ teaspoon fine salt

about 10 twists of black pepper

150g very ripe pineapple, cut into
    ¾ cm cubes

2 teaspoons lemon juice

To serve

180g friggitelli or Padrón
    peppers (optional)

olive oil

flaked salt

2 large burratas (optional)

good-quality prosciutto cotto/
    cooked ham (optional)

½ onion, thinly sliced on a mandolin

grilled focaccia or fried bread
    (page 179)

This pineapple salsa tastes like the distilled essence of a Hawaiian pizza (minus the ham, which you can absolutely serve with it if you like). I suggest serving it with burrata and charred green peppers such as friggitelli or Padrón, along with some grilled focaccia or Fried bread (page 179) to scoop it all up. You can also use the salsa as a condiment for burgers and sandwiches, or serve it alongside grilled fish or meat. I've tried to stick to the classic flavour profile of a Hawaiian pizza, but chipotle flakes would work really well alongside the regular chilli flakes, if you wanted to give the salsa a smoky edge.

Pancetta is a lovely addition to the salsa if you don't need it to be vegan and want it to taste even more like a Hawaiian pizza. Fry about 60g of pancetta cubes on a medium heat until beginning to crisp, then lower the heat and proceed with step 1. You should add a bit less oil if you've started with pancetta.

———————

Put all the ingredients for the salsa, except the pineapple and lemon juice, into a medium, non-stick frying pan. Place on a very low heat and cook for 5 minutes, stirring often. Remove from the heat and stir in the pineapple and lemon juice. Leave to infuse for 30 minutes before using.

If making the charred peppers, heat a large frying pan on a high heat. Once the pan is very hot, char the peppers for 2–3 minutes on each side, or until softened and nicely blackened in parts. Transfer to a bowl and toss with olive oil and flaked salt.

Spoon the pineapple salsa on a plate and top with the burratas (if using). Arrange the peppers and ham (if using) around the platter. Toss the onion together with some oil and flaked salt and scatter over the platter. Serve with grilled focaccia or fried bread to mop it all up.

Make ahead

The pineapple pizza salsa will keep for up to 2 weeks in the fridge.

Notes

An image of this recipe is on page 178.

60g crème fraîche or soured cream

60g mayonnaise

sriracha

olive oil, for frying

1 lime, cut into wedges, to serve

Fritters

1 very ripe plantain (soft, nearly all
    black with some yellow marks)

200g frozen corn, defrosted

2–3 spring onions, roughly chopped (30g)

2 cloves of garlic, finely grated/crushed

¾ teaspoon ground turmeric

⅛ teaspoon cayenne pepper

¼ teaspoon ground allspice (alternatively
    use ground cinnamon or ginger)

⅓ teaspoon fine salt

3 tablespoons plain flour
    (use gluten-free if you like)

3 large eggs

150g feta, broken into 1½ cm chunks

Plantain and corn fritters with sriracha mayo

Serve these fritters with eggs for breakfast, or stuff into a sandwich with some crunchy veg for textural contrast. Make sure the plantain you use is soft and very ripe – preferably nearly all black. If your plantain is not so ripe (and therefore not so sweet), add some maple syrup or honey to the mix.

———————

Leaving the skin on, cut the plantain widthways into thirds. Place in a medium saucepan and cover with boiling water. Cook on a medium heat until the plantain is very soft, about 15 minutes. Remove the skin and transfer the flesh to a sieve, letting any excess water drain away.

Pat the plantain dry, then put it into a food processor with the corn, spring onions, garlic, turmeric, cayenne, allspice and fine salt. Pulse a few times until the corn is roughly chopped – you're after a textured mixture, rather than a smooth one, so don't overmix it.

Transfer the mixture to a bowl. Stir in the flour and eggs until combined, then fold in the feta. Preheat the oven to 180°C fan/200°C.

Heat 1 tablespoon of oil in a large, non-stick frying pan on a medium-high heat. Once the oil is hot, spoon 80g of the mixture per fritter into the pan – the fritters should be about 7cm wide and you should be able to fit 4 or 5 in the pan at a time, spaced apart.

Immediately lower the heat to medium, then fry for 2–3 minutes on each side, or until golden-brown and crisp. Transfer to a flat baking tray and continue with the next batch, adding more oil as necessary.

When all the fritters are browned, transfer the tray to the oven for 5 minutes, until the fritters are cooked through.

Meanwhile, stir together the crème fraîche and mayo, then swirl through some sriracha to get streaks. Serve alongside the hot fritters, with lime wedges for squeezing over them.

450g good-quality gnocchi (I use
   Dell'ugo pumpkin gnocchi)
flaked salt

Roasted butternut

50g unsalted butter, cut into cubes
2 tablespoons olive oil
20g white miso paste
2 teaspoons maple syrup
2 teaspoons rose harissa
600g butternut squash, peeled and
   chopped into 3cm cubes
¼ teaspoon fine salt

Salsa

2 ripe tomatoes (230g)
¼–½ teaspoon Calabrian chilli paste
   (aka crema di pepperoncino) or
   hot sauce (optional)
½ clove of garlic, finely grated/crushed
1 teaspoon lemon juice
⅛ teaspoon fine salt

Za'atar butter

40g unsalted butter
2 tablespoons oil
1 tablespoon za'atar
1 small clove of garlic, very finely chopped
good pinch of fine salt

Vegan option

You can easily make this dish vegan
by using plant-based butter.

Make ahead

The butternut sauce will keep for up
to 2 days in the fridge.

Miso butter butternut gnocchi

You may have heard of miso butter onions … well, this is miso butter butternut, in which butternut squash gets roasted with miso, butter and harissa, then blitzed into a luxurious sauce to go with gnocchi or pasta. You could even pair the sauce with butter beans – 'nature's gnocchi' – in which case you could call it 'miso butter butternut butter beans' (please don't ever call it that). If you want to make gnocchi from scratch, there's a great recipe on page 94 of *Ottolenghi Flavour*, if you have a copy.

———

Preheat the oven to 220°C/240°C.

For the roasted butternut, place the butter, oil, miso, maple syrup, rose harissa, butternut and salt into a high-sided baking tray just big enough to fit everything in a single layer (but not too large that everything is really spread out). Cover with foil and bake for 20 minutes. Remove the foil, stir and bake for another 10 minutes, until soft, golden-brown and bubbling. Spoon the contents of the tray into a blender and blitz until completely smooth. It should all be soft enough to blend, but add a splash of water if needed.

For the salsa, halve the tomatoes and grate the flesh sides into a bowl using the large holes of a box grater – you should have 140g. Discard the tomato skins and stir in the chilli paste (if using), garlic, lemon juice and salt.

For the za'atar butter, place the butter and oil in a medium frying pan on a medium heat and cook for 2–3 minutes until the butter melts and begins to brown. Remove from the heat and stir in the za'atar, garlic and a good pinch of salt.

Cook the gnocchi per packet instructions in salted boiling water. Transfer the cooked gnocchi to a sauté pan with the butternut sauce and 2–3 tablespoons of the gnocchi cooking water. Place on a medium heat and cook for 2 minutes, tossing to combine, until warm.

Transfer the gnocchi to a platter and top with the salsa, followed by the za'atar butter. Finish with flaked salt and serve.

2 aubergines, cut into 2cm chunks (500g)

350g sweet, ripe cherry tomatoes,
    such as Datterini

3 large mild red chillies, chopped
    into 3cm-long pieces (optional)

100g olive oil

1 teaspoon fine salt

125g buffalo mozzarella, roughly
    torn into chunks (optional)

freshly ground black pepper

Coriander and anchovy salsa

2 cloves of garlic, very finely chopped

3 anchovy fillets in olive oil, very
    finely chopped (alternatively
    use green olives)

5g fresh coriander, finely chopped

5g fresh basil, finely chopped,
    plus extra leaves to garnish

4 tablespoons olive oil

1 teaspoon lemon juice

Roasted aubergines with coriander and anchovy salsa

There are plenty of options with this warm salad: scoop it up with some grilled bread, stir it through pasta or serve it on top of polenta. It's especially good with the fried pizza bread on page 179.

———

Preheat the oven to 210°C fan/230°C and line a large, flat baking tray with parchment paper.

Mix the aubergines with the tomatoes, chillies, oil, fine salt and plenty of pepper. Spread them out as much as possible across the tray. If the vegetables are snug they'll stew in their own juices and won't take on any colour!

Roast for about 45 minutes, stirring halfway through, until the aubergines are a dark golden-brown and the tomatoes are soft. Set aside to cool a little.

Stir all the ingredients for the salsa together in a small bowl.

Transfer the roasted veg to a platter. Top with the mozzarella, if using, then spoon over the salsa. Finish with the basil leaves and serve warm.

250g dried orzo pasta

500g water

300g silken tofu, drained (290g)

80g baby spinach

¾ tablespoon olive oil

½ lemon

2 tablespoons fresh chives or spring
    onions, finely chopped, to serve

fine salt

Piri piri sauce

150g sweet, ripe cherry tomatoes, such as
    Datterini, very finely chopped to a pulp

1 tablespoon tomato purée/paste

1 teaspoon smoked paprika

up to 1 tablespoon piri piri seasoning
    (or use Cajun seasoning as an
    alternative)

4 tablespoons olive oil, plus extra to serve

2 cloves of garlic, very finely chopped

2 teaspoons lemon juice

½ teaspoon fine salt

about 15 twists of freshly ground
    black pepper

Piri piri tofu over crispy crispy orzo

This simple dish ticks a few important boxes: it's vegan, it's one pan, and it's also a meal-in-one, featuring protein, carbs and veg. If all goes to plan, the bottom layer of orzo should be nice and crispy. If you don't need it to be vegan, fish cut into 2½cm cubes or whole, peeled king prawns would make lovely alternatives to the silken tofu.

Piri piri seasonings tend to be quite spicy, so use less if you prefer milder heat.

––––––––

First make the piri piri sauce. Mix all the ingredients together in a medium bowl (add less piri piri seasoning at first if you don't like too much heat). Put half the sauce into a 28cm sauté pan with the orzo and water. Mix together and set aside.

Cut the tofu into 2½cm cubes and add to the bowl with the remaining piri piri sauce. Sprinkle with a good pinch of salt, then very gently stir together so the tofu is coated. Set aside.

Place the pan with the orzo and water on a medium-high heat. Cook for 8–9 minutes, stirring continuously, until most of the water has been absorbed and the orzo is al dente. Remove from the heat.

Flatten the surface of the orzo. Spoon the tofu and sauce evenly over the cooked orzo. Mix the spinach with the ¾ tablespoon of oil and a good pinch of fine salt, then arrange over the top.

Cover the pan with a lid and return to a medium heat. Cook for 5 minutes, then remove the lid and cook for another 3–4 minutes, or until the liquid that was produced when steaming the spinach has been reabsorbed, and the bottom of the orzo is crispy. Leave to cool for 5 minutes.

Move the spinach to reveal the tofu pieces below. Squeeze over some lemon juice, then finish with the chives and a good drizzle of oil.

Make ahead

The piri piri sauce will keep for up to a week in the fridge.

280g Roasted onion aïoli (page 139)

4 thick slices of good bread,
    such as focaccia or sourdough

1 large clove of garlic, peeled and halved

2–3 very ripe tomatoes, sliced

young pecorino or Parmesan, thinly sliced

1 tablespoon fresh chives, finely chopped

5g fresh basil leaves

very good extra virgin olive oil

flaked salt

freshly ground black pepper

Roasted onion aïoli and tomato toast

This is another use for the Roasted onion aioli on page 139, but it's more of a blueprint than a recipe – feel free to get creative with what you pair the aioli with.

———

First make the aioli on page 139.

Place a grill pan on a high heat and once very hot, grill the bread for about 2 minutes on each side, or until you get clear grill marks. Alternatively, use a toaster, or toast the bread under your oven grill.

Rub each piece of grilled bread with plenty of raw garlic, then leave to cool for a few minutes.

Spread a generous amount of aïoli over the bread, about 70g per slice. Top with the tomatoes, then season generously with flaked salt and plenty of pepper.

Top with the pecorino and herbs, and finish with plenty of very good olive oil.

3 onions, halved and thinly sliced
    on a mandolin (480g)

6 tablespoons olive oil

1 teaspoon fine salt

2 x 400g tins of Puy, brown or green
    lentils in salted water, drained (440g)

70g water or chicken/veg stock

50g white wine

¼ teaspoon ground cumin

1 tablespoon soy sauce

Caramelised onion aïoli

1 teaspoon white miso paste

¼ teaspoon English mustard

100g plant-based or regular milk

2 tablespoons olive oil

2 teaspoons lemon juice

To serve

shop-bought crispy chilli oil
    (or use the Numbing oil recipe from
    Ottolenghi Flavour, page 196, if you
    have a copy)

1 tablespoon fresh chives, parsley
    or coriander, finely chopped

2 lemons, halved

Make ahead

The onion aïoli will keep in the fridge
for 3 days.

Notes

If starting with dried lentils, put 200g
into a large saucepan and cover with
well-salted water. Bring to a simmer over
a medium-high heat, then lower the heat
and cook for 25–30 minutes, or until the
lentils are soft but still have some bite.
Drain, then proceed with the recipe.

This image also shows Caldo de feijão
with spicy pine nut oil, see page 84.

Lentils with caramelised onion aïoli and crispy chilli oil

Tinned lentils are given star treatment when paired with an addictive (vegan) caramelised onion aïoli (for want of a better description) and crispy chilli oil. The only bit of hands-on cooking is frying the onions, which admittedly does take some time, but is well worth it. You can get ahead by frying a bunch of onions up to 2 weeks in advance and keeping a stash in the fridge. My fridge is almost never without a container of deeply caramelised onions, which I add to soups, broths, stews and sauces, thereby effortlessly increasing flavour. I encourage you to fry off a bunch of onions every few weeks, and to thank me later.

The caramelised onion aïoli is a great condiment in its own right – use it in sandwiches and burgers, spoon it into soups, or serve it alongside roast chicken.

————

Put the onions, 5 tablespoons of the oil and ¾ teaspoon of fine salt into a large sauté pan on a medium heat. Fry for 22–26 minutes, stirring often, until deeply golden and caramelised. Make sure you don't let the onions burn, or the aïoli will be bitter – lower the heat if the onions are colouring too quickly.

To make the aïoli, transfer 90g of the caramelised onions to a blender while still warm. Add the miso, mustard, milk, olive oil and lemon juice and blitz until smooth, scraping down the sides as needed.

Put the rest of the onions (about 60g) into a small bowl and set aside to serve.

Put the drained lentils into the pan you fried the onions in. Add the water, wine, cumin, soy sauce, the remaining 1 tablespoon of olive oil and ¼ teaspoon of fine salt. Place on a medium-high heat and cook for 4 minutes, or until bubbling and hot.

Divide the lentils between two bowls and top with a generous spoonful of the onion aïoli. Drizzle over some chilli oil, then top with the remaining caramelised onions. Finish with the herbs and a squeeze of lemon, and serve.

2 x 400g tins of black beans in
    salted water
crème fraîche or soured cream
    (optional, use plant-based to
    keep the dish vegan)
2 spring onions, green ends thinly
    sliced, to serve
1 lime, cut into wedges, to serve

Spicy pine nut oil
20g pine nuts
½ onion, very finely chopped (60g)
¼ teaspoon fine salt
4 tablespoons olive oil
1 small clove of garlic, finely
    grated/crushed
1 teaspoon smoked mild paprika
1 teaspoon hot sauce, such as
    Kold Sauce or Tabasco (optional)
1 teaspoon tomato purée/paste
⅛ teaspoon ground cumin
⅛ teaspoon ground cinnamon

Caldo de feijão with spicy pine nut oil

Caldo de feijão – bean broth – is a Brazilian dish (really more of a textured soup than a broth) usually made with black turtle beans and sometimes with brown pinto beans. This soup is very close to my heart, it's my kind of chicken soup for the soul. When I lived in Rio with my oldest best friend, Roma, we would often end up at our favourite Bar do Mineiro in Santa Teresa on rainy days. Our order was always the same: a bowl each of *caldo de feijão* topped with spicy cubes of smoked pork, and a basket of *pastéis de camarão* (prawn pasties) to share, doused with hot sauce.

This is a simplified version that uses tinned beans for ease. It's enhanced by an addictive spicy pine nut oil, which is reminiscent of the flavours of the smoked pork often served with *caldo de feijão*, but without the meat. You can of course add smoked pork if you like. Fry about 60g of smoked lardons or pancetta cubes on a medium heat until beginning to brown before adding the rest of the ingredients and proceeding with step 1. Add less oil if you've started with pancetta.

The crème fraîche is both untraditional and optional.

————

For the oil, put the pine nuts, onion, fine salt and 2 tablespoons of the olive oil into a medium frying pan and place on a medium heat. Fry for about 5 minutes, stirring often, until the onions and pine nuts are beginning to turn golden. Turn the heat down to low and continue to fry for 3 minutes, stirring often, or until the onions are a deep golden-brown.

Remove from the heat, then stir in the garlic, paprika, hot sauce, tomato purée/paste, cumin, cinnamon, the remaining 2 tablespoons of oil and another pinch of salt.

Tip the beans along with their salted water into a blender and pulse a couple of times, just to roughly chop them (you're not after a smooth soup). Add salt to taste (especially if your beans were unsalted). Transfer to a saucepan and place on a medium-high heat for a few minutes, until hot.

Divide the soup between four bowls and top with a spoonful of crème fraîche (optional). Spoon over some of the pine nut oil and finish with the spring onions. Squeeze over some lime juice and serve.

Notes
An image of this recipe is on page 82.

FISH

Each salad serves 2

2 gem lettuces, halved lengthways

2 teaspoons olive oil

flaked salt

Dill roasted tomatoes

400g sweet, ripe cherry tomatoes,
    such as Datterini

20g fresh dill, stalks and leaves

3 cloves of garlic, peeled and crushed
    with the side of a knife

70g olive oil

1½ teaspoons maple syrup or honey

1¼ teaspoons caraway seeds

1 teaspoon flaked salt

Tuna crema

80g tinned tuna in olive oil (don't
    drain away the oil) (see notes
    for vegetarian version)

2 anchovies in olive oil

10g Parmesan, finely grated

½ teaspoon English mustard

½ small clove of garlic

1 tablespoon lemon juice

60g single cream

Jalapeño cucumber salsa

½ cucumber, peeled, halved and
    watery centre scraped out

5g fresh chives

5g fresh dill

1 jalapeño

2 tablespoons olive oil

¾ teaspoon flaked salt

1 tablespoon lemon juice

Notes

For a vegetarian version of the tuna crema,
use a vegetarian Parmesan alternative,
replace the anchovies with white miso
paste, and instead of the tuna, use 80g of
pitted nocellara olives plus ½ tablespoon
of olive oil. Use a plant-based cream if you
want to make a vegan version.

Charred gem lettuce two ways

Calling this recipe 'Charred gem lettuce two ways' is really just a sneaky way of getting in an extra recipe, since I didn't want to have to choose between the two (which is why even though this recipe is in the **FISH** section, there's also a veg version). Here the charred gem lettuce and jalapeño cucumber salsa are the constants, and the base is interchangeable depending on your mood. Option one is a tuna crema, which I wouldn't dream of calling *tonnato* as it has cream and Parmesan in it and no egg. Option two is cherry tomatoes roasted with dill and caraway seeds. Both options work incredibly well with charred gem lettuce, which incidentally is such a delicious way of preparing lettuce that you may never want to eat it raw again. I'd highly recommend making both versions and serving them alongside each other.

—————

Preheat the oven to 230°C fan/250°C if you're making the roasted tomatoes. You won't need the oven for the tuna version.

For the tomatoes, put all the ingredients into an ovenproof dish that's just big enough to fit them all snugly in a single layer. Stir, then roast for 30 minutes on the top shelf of the oven.

For the tuna crema, put all the ingredients (including the oil from the tuna tin) into a blender and blitz until smooth.

For the jalapeño cucumber salsa, thinly slice the cucumber at an angle. Very finely chop the herbs and jalapeño, then put them into a bowl with the oil, salt and cucumber. Don't add the lemon juice until you're ready to serve.

Heat a large frying pan on a high heat. Season the cut sides of each lettuce half with ½ teaspoon oil and ¼ teaspoon flaked salt.

Once the pan is very hot, arrange the lettuce halves cut side down in the pan and char for about 3½–4 minutes, pressing down on the lettuce with a spatula to create an even char.

Spoon either the tuna crema or the roasted tomatoes on to a platter and top with the charred lettuce. Stir the lemon juice into the cucumber salsa, spoon on top of the lettuce and serve.

Dendê marinated prawns with burnt lime

350g extra large, raw peeled
    king prawns (about 700g
    if starting with whole prawns shell on)
2 limes, halved
2 tablespoons sunflower or light olive oil

Dendê marinade

80g red palm oil (aka *azeite de dendê*,
    page 15 for more info and subs)
80g ghee (from a jar not a tin, see page 17)
    or unsalted butter, softened
30g fresh ginger, peeled and
    roughly chopped
6 large cloves of garlic,
    roughly chopped (25g)
½ medium onion, roughly chopped (60g)
2 mild red chillies, deseeded
    and roughly chopped (20g)
2 Scotch bonnet chillies, deseeded
    and roughly chopped (optional
    or start with less and add more
    to taste)
1½ tablespoons lime juice
4 teaspoons tomato purée/paste
1½ teaspoons caster sugar
1 teaspoon chipotle flakes
2 teaspoons fine salt

Notes

If you don't have a food processor/
blender, pound the ginger, garlic, onion,
chillies and fine salt with a pestle and
mortar to get a rough paste, then mix with
the remaining marinade ingredients.

This image also shows Creamed plantain
with dendê, ginger and lime, see page 65.

This marinade, featuring *azeite de dendê* (page 15), ginger and Scotch bonnet among other delights, is one of my favourites in the book. It works particularly well as a marinade for things that cook quickly, so it keeps its freshness and vibrancy: prawns, chunks of fish and cubes of marinated tofu, for example. It's also great as a punchy condiment (no need to cook) in sandwiches and burgers, or it can be melted over grilled corn on the cob.

You'll make more marinade than you need, but it keeps for up to a week in the fridge. Use 80g of the leftover marinade to make the Creamed plantain on page 65, which is pictured here and goes perfectly with the prawns.

For the dendê marinade, put the palm oil and ghee into a small saucepan on a medium-low heat and cook until just melted. Leave to cool for a few minutes, then transfer to a small food processor or blender with all the remaining ingredients for the marinade. Pulse to get a rough paste, scraping down the sides as needed.

Run a small, sharp knife down the back of each prawn to slightly butterfly them open, and de-vein them if necessary. Put them into a bowl with 120g of the marinade, mix well and set aside to marinate for 5 minutes.

If you're making the Creamed plantain (page 65), do this before you start frying the prawns.

Heat a large, non-stick frying pan on a high heat. Once very hot, place the lime halves in the pan, cut side down, and cook until charred, about 3 minutes. Transfer the limes to a plate, cut side up.

Keep the pan on a high heat and add 2 tablespoons of sunflower oil. Add the prawns and quickly spread them out as much as possible. If your pan is small, you'll need to cook them in two batches so you don't overcrowd the pan. Fry for 2 minutes, turning halfway, until nicely browned on both sides but only *just* cooked. Remove the pan from the heat and stir another 2 tablespoons of the marinade into the prawns, until melted.

Transfer to a large plate with the burnt lime. Serve with grilled bread, for mopping up all the oil, or with Creamed plantain if you've made it.

70g olive oil

4 cloves of garlic, peeled and crushed
    with the side of a knife

1 Scotch bonnet chilli, whole
    and unpierced (optional)

200g sweet, ripe cherry tomatoes,
    such as Datterini, halved

1 teaspoon tomato purée/paste

½ teaspoon sweet paprika

½ teaspoon fine salt

10g fresh basil leaves

70g white wine

800g clams

200g jarred chickpeas or beans (optional)

5g fresh chives, finely chopped

2 lemons: 2 tablespoons lemon juice
    and the rest cut into wedges

2 tablespoons double cream (optional)

1 jalapeño, thinly sliced (optional)

freshly ground black pepper

A very quick clam stew

There is possibly nothing more delicious than brothy, garlicky, oily clams. Clams are your friends! They are incredibly quick to cook, incredibly easy to get right and they *still* always manage to impress. The chickpeas are optional – you can also toss the clams with pasta instead, or serve them with grilled bread or chips.

––––––––––

Put the first seven ingredients, half the basil and plenty of pepper into a large sauté pan on a medium-high heat. Fry for 4 minutes, stirring often.

Add the wine, followed by the clams spread out as much as possible, and bring to a simmer. Once gently simmering, cover with a lid, turn the heat down to medium-low and cook for about 5 minutes, or until all or most of the clams have opened. Discard any clams that don't open. Discard the Scotch bonnet, squeezing it into the sauce first if you like heat. Stir in the chickpeas (if using), the chives and lemon juice.

Serve from the pan or transfer to a lipped platter. Drizzle over the cream (if using), then top with the jalapeño and the remaining basil leaves, and serve with lemon wedges.

1kg roasting potatoes, skin on
and cut into 1cm-thick chips
3 tablespoons olive oil, plus extra to serve
2 teaspoons flaked salt
160g tin of tuna in olive oil, drained
5g fresh chives, roughly chopped
5g fresh basil leaves
freshly ground black pepper

Pickled onions
½ onion, thinly sliced on a mandolin
2 tablespoons lemon juice
½ teaspoon flaked salt

Parmesan cream
4 tablespoons double cream
15g Parmesan, finely grated,
plus extra to serve
½ clove of garlic, crushed
flaked salt

Scotch bonnet salsa
2 ripe tomatoes (170g)
½ Scotch bonnet chilli, finely chopped
(use a milder chilli if you prefer)
½ teaspoon hot sauce (optional)
½ clove of garlic, finely grated/crushed
flaked salt

Make ahead
The Parmesan cream and Scotch bonnet
salsa will keep for up to 2 days in the fridge.
Bring them back to room temperature
before using.

TV chips

These loaded chips are best eaten in front of the TV. Although I assure you that this is a tried and tested fact, I also invite you to try and test for yourself. Less of a recipe and more of a blueprint, these chips are a foundation on which to build your own vision. I've loaded mine with tuna, Parmesan cream and Scotch bonnet salsa, but the possibilities are endless. Try them loaded with roast chicken and curry sauce (page 222), with salsa roja (page 24) and pickled onions, or with Mexicorn sauce and spring onion salsa (page 213).

Your baking tray needs to be flat, not high-sided, otherwise the potatoes will steam rather than crisp. A kilo of potatoes is really the maximum you should be putting on a tray – any more and you'll have to start piling the chips up, when really you want them to be spread out as much as possible, to crisp up and colour evenly.

Preheat the oven to 220°C fan/240°C.

Line the largest flat baking tray that will fit in your oven with parchment paper. Toss the chips with the oil and salt and spread them out as much as possible on the tray. Bake for 20 minutes, then lower the heat to 200°C fan/220°C and use the parchment to help you gently toss the chips. Bake for another 20 minutes or so – keep an eye on them for the last 5 minutes and take them out when they're at your ideal level of golden-brown.

Meanwhile, mix the onions with the lemon juice and salt, and set aside.

Stir the cream with the Parmesan, garlic and a pinch of salt, and set aside.

Halve and grate the cut sides of the tomatoes using the large holes of a box grater. Discard the skin, and put the pulp into a small bowl with the Scotch bonnet, hot sauce (if using) and garlic. Add 1 tablespoon of the pickling liquid from the onions and a pinch of salt, and stir.

Assemble! Spread your hot chips out on a platter and top with chunks of the tuna. Spoon over the cream and salsa, layering with the pickled onions (and some of the pickling liquid), chives and basil. Finish with extra virgin olive oil, black pepper and a final grating of Parmesan.

4 x 100g skinless and boneless hake fillets
(see notes for alternatives)
1 tablespoon lime juice
1 teaspoon fine salt
2 tablespoons coconut oil
10 fresh lime leaves (5g)
5g fresh Thai basil leaves,
plus extra to serve
400g tin of full-fat coconut milk
(at least 70% coconut extract)
3 tablespoons water
300g straight-to-wok fresh udon noodles
(not the dried variety)
1 lime, cut into wedges, to serve

Tomato turmeric sambal

4 mild red chillies, roughly chopped
(deseeded if you prefer less heat)
150g sweet, ripe cherry tomatoes,
such as Datterini
10g fresh turmeric, peeled
10g fresh ginger, peeled
2 cloves of garlic, peeled
½ small onion (70g)
1½ teaspoons black peppercorns,
roughly crushed
1 teaspoon fine salt
2 tablespoons maple syrup or honey
20g lime juice

Make ahead

The sambal will keep for up to a week
in the fridge.

Notes

You can use any white, meaty fish here.
Cod, hake, pollock and halibut are all
good options. The noodles and sauce
are also great with leftover roast chicken
(page 222) instead of fish.

Fish poached in tomato and turmeric curry with udon noodles

This recipe is inspired by a few different dishes. The sambal is loosely based on Indonesian *sambal tomat*, while the finished dish could be likened to Indonesian *laksa* or Thai *khao soi*, in the way that the noodles are cooked in a fragrant coconut-based curry (although the flavours are very different). The result is a quick, one-pan meal that I hope will become one of those go-to recipes you know like the back of your hand. Serve with marinated tofu instead of fish for a vegan version.

I highly recommend having a stash of the sambal in your fridge at all times. Use it as a base for curries, as a condiment for roasted and grilled meats, fish and veg, or to make fried rice.

———————

First marinate the fish with the lime juice and 1 teaspoon of fine salt. Mix to coat, then set aside while you prepare the rest, or for up to an hour.

For the sambal, put all the ingredients into a blender and blitz until combined, but not completely smooth.

Heat the coconut oil in a large sauté pan or wok on a high heat. Once melted, add the lime leaves and basil leaves and stir-fry for 1 minute. Add half the sambal and stir-fry for about 4 minutes, until thickened and deep red, then add the rest of the sambal and stir-fry for another 4 minutes. Turn the heat down a bit if it's spitting.

Add the coconut milk and water, stir together and simmer for 2 minutes.

Stir the noodles into the curry sauce so they are submerged, then place the fish fillets on top, spooning over some of the sauce. Cover with a lid, turn the heat down to medium and cook for 4–5 minutes, or until the fish is *just* cooked. Remove from the heat, leaving the lid on for another 3 minutes.

Garnish with Thai basil and serve with the lime wedges on the side.

Serves 4

3–4 ripe yellow tomatoes (180g)

3–4 ripe green tomatoes or
   tomatillos (180g)

¾ teaspoon flaked salt

4 x 80–120g plaice fillets
   (or 2 larger fillets)

½ lemon

½ lime

olive oil

fine salt

fresh oregano leaves, to serve

fresh basil leaves, to serve

Chilli and garlic butter

40g unsalted butter

3 tablespoons olive oil

2–3 large, mild red chillies, deseeded if
   you like, thinly sliced into rounds (20g)

¼ teaspoon fine salt

2 large (or 3 medium) cloves of garlic,
   very finely chopped (not crushed!)

Notes

Lemon sole or smaller sea bream/sea
bass fillets will also work here, but may
need to cook for longer.

If you don't like heat, skip the part where
you fry the chillies and just warm the
butter and oil before adding the garlic.
Add a small pinch of chilli flakes, if you
like mild heat.

Plaice with yellow and green tomatoes

Something beautiful happens when the natural juices of the tomatoes, citrus and fish come together with the garlic and chilli butter, and you'll want some good bread on hand to capture the moment. This is the ultimate midweek summer dish, as it only takes 10 minutes to make. As ever, make sure your tomatoes are nice and ripe, it'll make all the difference. If you can get hold of tomatillos, these are lovely in place of green tomatoes. Of course, you can also use good-quality red tomatoes, if that's what's more readily available.

—————

Preheat the oven to the highest grill setting.

Slice the tomatoes and arrange on a large serving platter. Sprinkle with ¾ teaspoon of flaked salt and set aside while you cook the fish.

Pat the plaice fillets dry and place on a flat baking tray, skin side down and spaced apart. Rub the flesh side with a good drizzle of oil and a generous sprinkle of salt. Grill on the top shelf of the oven until opaque and *just* cooked (you're not looking to brown the fillets). This should take about 1 minute per 20g. So, a 60g fillet should take about 3 minutes, a 120g fillet about 6 minutes, a 180g fillet about 9 minutes and so on, however this will also depend on your grill as some are much hotter than others. You want the fish to be *just* cooked and no longer translucent. Use a wide spatula to carefully transfer the fish to the platter of tomatoes.

For the chilli and garlic butter, put the butter and oil into a medium non-stick frying pan on a medium heat. Once melted, add the chillies and salt and fry for 2½ minutes, swirling the pan, until the chillies are bright red and crisp (lower the heat if they are browning too quickly). Transfer to a small bowl to stop them cooking, then stir in the finely chopped garlic. Leave to infuse for a few minutes.

Squeeze the lemon and lime halves over the fish and tomatoes, then spoon the chilli and garlic butter all over. Sprinkle generously with flaked salt, top with some fresh oregano and basil and serve.

Serves 4

1kg mussels

80g dried orzo pasta

30g unsalted butter (or another
    2 tablespoons olive oil)

2 tablespoons olive oil

½ small onion, finely chopped

4 cloves of garlic, very finely
    chopped (not crushed!)

1 yellow pepper, chopped into
    1cm pieces (120g)

1 Scotch bonnet chilli, whole
    and unpierced (or a milder
    chilli if you prefer)

1¼ teaspoons fine salt

150g sweet yellow cherry tomatoes,
    roughly chopped

½ teaspoon tomato purée/paste

¾ teaspoon saffron threads

400g tin of full-fat coconut milk
    (at least 70% coconut extract)

up to 2 teaspoons Calabrian chilli paste
    aka crema di pepperoncino, to serve
    (optional, see intro for alternatives)

1 lemon, halved

Herb oil

5g fresh chives, finely chopped

5g fresh coriander, finely chopped

3 tablespoons olive oil

⅛ teaspoon fine salt

Mussels and orzo in a coconut and saffron stew

This dish is deceptively simple despite the longish method. Mussels go perfectly with the saffron, Scotch bonnet and coconut stew, but if you're not so keen on them, you could use clams, prawns or pieces of fish instead. You'll need to add a splash of water if using prawns or fish, as mussels create quite a lot of liquid. I like to stir through a couple of teaspoons of Calabrian chilli paste before serving (Seggiano is my go-to brand). If you can't get hold of any, use the Scotch bonnet salsa on page 31.

––––––––––

Put the mussels into a large bowl and cover with cold water. Debeard them by pulling any tufty bits up towards the top of the shell, and then out. Discard any shells that are open or cracked.

Put the orzo into a medium bowl and cover with boiling water. Set aside for 15 minutes, then drain and rinse.

Meanwhile, put the butter and oil into a large sauté pan (you'll need a lid for it later) and place it on a medium-low heat. Once melted, add the onion, garlic, yellow pepper, Scotch bonnet (if using) and fine salt. Gently fry for 8 minutes, stirring often, until the onions and garlic are soft and fragrant. You don't want them to crisp or brown too much, so turn the heat down if necessary.

Increase the heat to medium and add the chopped yellow tomatoes, tomato purée/paste and saffron. Stir-fry for 2 minutes, then stir in the coconut milk and simmer for 3 minutes.

Add the orzo to the stew, followed by the mussels in a layer on top. Cover with a lid and turn the heat all the way down. Cook for 5 minutes, or until all the shells have opened.

Discard the Scotch bonnet, if using, squeezing it into the sauce first if you like heat. Taste the sauce and stir in up to 2 teaspoons of Calabrian chilli paste to taste, if you like heat.

Squeeze plenty of lemon juice over the mussels. Mix all the ingredients for the herb oil together, spoon over the mussels and serve.

6 crumpets (or tostadas/sourdough toast)

40g ghee (from a jar not a tin, see page 17)
    or unsalted butter

20g soy sauce

200g sashimi-grade tuna

fine salt

1 lime, cut into wedges, to serve

Cucumber salsa

1 cucumber, peeled, halved and watery
    centre scraped out (200g)

1½ tablespoons lime juice

1½ teaspoons flaked salt

10g fresh chives, very finely chopped

5g fresh coriander, very finely chopped

1 jalapeño, very finely chopped (optional)

3 tablespoons olive oil

Tuna crudo crumpets with soy butter

This would make an impressive starter, but could just as easily be a quick and indulgent midweek dinner. Feel free to swap the tuna for another sashimi-grade fish – raw scallop also works well. I love the bubbly texture of the crumpet here, but you could also use tostadas or toasted sourdough for the base.

———————

For the salsa, cut the cucumber into 1cm cubes. Mix the cucumber, lime and salt together and leave to pickle for 20 minutes to 3 hours. Drain well and discard the liquid.

Place the chives, coriander, jalapeno (if using) and oil in a medium bowl with the drained pickled cucumber. Mix together and set aside.

Toast the crumpets well (I tend to toast them twice) until golden-brown and crisp on top.

Put the ghee and soy sauce into a small saucepan on a medium heat and gently cook until the ghee has melted.

With a sharp knife, slice the tuna into 1cm cubes. Season with a pinch of fine salt.

Pile the tuna on top of the crumpets, then spoon over a generous amount of the soy butter. Top with some of the cucumber and serve with the lime wedges.

Notes
Cucumber avocado is a great addition
to the salsa, if you have some.

The method here might seem slightly long to be in **EVERYDAY**, but it's really very straightforward – the kind of recipe you'll only need to follow once before recreating from intuition and memory. Cod, hake and pollock are all good options here. If using thinner fillets like sea bass or sea bream, cook them for a minute or two less. If you don't want to make aïoli from scratch, stir paprika and saffron through a couple of large spoonfuls of shop-bought mayo.

First marinate the fish with the lime juice and fine salt. Mix to coat, then set aside while you prepare the rest, or for up to 3 hours.

If making the aïoli, put the egg yolks, fine salt, garlic, paprika, black pepper and saffron into a medium bowl and whisk until smooth and combined. Add half the oil and whisk vigorously for 30 seconds, until it is fully incorporated and the mixture begins to thicken. Add the remaining half of the oil and whisk vigorously again for about a minute, or as long as your arm can handle, then stir in the vinegar. This isn't a particularly thick aïoli, so no need to lose an arm over it. Set aside.

Heat a large sauté pan on a high heat. Once the pan is smoking hot, add the tomatoes and the Scotch bonnet and cook for about 6 minutes, shaking the pan every now and then, until the tomatoes are nicely charred in parts.

Remove the pan from the heat and add the fine salt, oil, garlic, paprika, tomato purée/paste and half each of the coriander and basil.

Mix well, then return to a medium heat and stir-fry for 2 minutes. Add the water and butter and bring to a simmer. Simmer gently for 5 minutes, squeezing most of the tomatoes into the broth. Nestle the fish fillets into the broth, cover with a lid or a larger pan and cook for 3 minutes, or until opaque and just cooked through (larger fillets will of course take longer). Remove from the heat, leaving the lid on for another 2 minutes.

Discard the Scotch bonnet (or squeeze it into the broth if you like heat). Top with the jalapeño, if using, olives and remaining herbs. Serve with the aïoli spooned on top and with lime wedges and grilled bread alongside.

Marinated fish

4 x 100g skinless and boneless
    fish fillets
1 tablespoon lime juice
1 teaspoon fine salt

Paprika aïoli
(optional – see recipe intro)

3 good-quality egg yolks
¼ teaspoon fine salt
½ small clove of garlic, crushed
¼ teaspoon sweet paprika
pinch of saffron (optional)
50g light olive oil (not extra virgin,
    that will be too strong here)
½ teaspoon rice vinegar or lime juice
freshly ground black pepper

Broth

250g sweet, ripe cherry tomatoes,
    such as Datterini
1 Scotch bonnet chilli, whole
    and unpierced (or a milder
    chilli if you prefer)
½ teaspoon fine salt
5 tablespoons olive oil
3 cloves of garlic, very finely
    chopped (not crushed!)
½ teaspoon paprika
1 tablespoon tomato purée/paste
5g fresh coriander, plus extra to garnish
5g fresh basil, plus extra to garnish
350g water
15g unsalted butter
1 jalapeño or green chilli, thinly
    sliced into rounds (optional)
70g Nocellara olives (or another
    green olive), pitted and roughly
    chopped (50g)
1–2 limes, cut into wedges, to serve
grilled bread, to serve (optional)

1 medium cucumber, peeled, halved
    and watery centre scraped out
1 teaspoon flaked salt
2½ tablespoons lime juice
300g straight-to-wok fresh udon noodles
    (not the dried variety)
2 x 115g tins of mackerel in olive oil,
    drained (or use marinated tofu)
2 spring onions, thinly sliced
2 teaspoons sesame seeds, toasted
    (I like to use a mix of black and white)
1 lime, cut into wedges, to serve

Dressing

5 tablespoons mild and light olive oil
    or sunflower oil
40g ginger, peeled and julienned
2 large mild red chillies, finely
    sliced into rounds (deseeded
    if you prefer less heat)
2 whole star anise
1 cinnamon stick, bashed with
    the side of a knife
2 tablespoons soy sauce
1½ tablespoons maple syrup
¾ teaspoon toasted sesame oil

Mackerel udon

I love mackerel in all forms, and tinned mackerel is one of my favourite go-to cupboard ingredients when I need a quick dinner. This recipe is inspired by a simple and delicious tinned mackerel stir-fry my friend Joe made for me a few times. I've complicated this version somewhat by adding pickled cucumber and crispy aromatics, but it's still very straightforward. Use marinated tofu instead of the mackerel to keep this dish vegan. I like the noodles to be at room temperature here, but you can serve them warm if you prefer.

———————

Cut the cucumber into ½cm-thick diagonal slices. In a medium bowl, mix the cucumber with the flaked salt and the lime juice. Set aside to pickle while you make the rest, or for up to 1 hour.

In a large bowl, cover the noodles with boiling water and leave for 5 minutes, then drain well and set aside while you make the dressing.

Prepare a heatproof sieve set over a heatproof bowl. Put the oil for the dressing into a medium saucepan on a medium heat. Once hot, add the ginger, chillies, star anise and cinnamon and gently fry, stirring often to separate the aromatics, until the ginger is crisp and golden. This will take about 5 minutes but watch closely, as the ginger can turn from golden to burned quite quickly. Drain through the sieve, collecting the aromatic oil in the bowl beneath. Set the crispy aromatics aside.

Transfer 3 tablespoons of the aromatic oil to a separate bowl along with the soy sauce, maple syrup and sesame oil. Use any remaining oil for another recipe.

Drain the cucumbers, then toss together with the noodles. Transfer to a lipped platter, then top with the tinned mackerel. Spoon over the dressing, followed by the crispy aromatics, spring onions and sesame seeds. Squeeze over some lime juice and serve.

1 x 800g sea bass, at room temperature

2 stalks of fresh rosemary

40g spring onions (about 4 thin ones)

fine salt

1 baby gem lettuce, leaves separated

5g fresh mint leaves

5g fresh coriander leaves

5g fresh basil leaves

lime wedges

Citrus butter

40g unsalted butter

30g olive oil

1½ tablespoons tangerine juice

2 teaspoons lime juice

3 cloves of garlic, skin left on and
    crushed with the side of a knife

1 teaspoon fine salt

about 20 twists of freshly ground
    black pepper

Tangerine dipping sauce

1½ teaspoons pul biber (use red bell
    pepper flakes if you don't like heat)

1 small clove of garlic, finely chopped

¼ teaspoon finely grated fresh ginger

¾ teaspoon tomato purée/paste

¼ teaspoon fine salt

1½ tablespoons mild and light olive oil

40g sweet, ripe cherry tomatoes, such as
    Datterini, very finely chopped

4 tablespoons tangerine juice

2 teaspoons lime juice

¼ teaspoon fish sauce or light soy sauce

Make ahead

The dipping sauce can be made up
to 2 days ahead.

Notes

The sticky coconut rice cake on page 124
(without the tomatoes) is a great addition
to this spread if you want to bulk things up.

Brown butter sea bass with tangerine dipping sauce and lots of herbs

Don't be put off by the longish ingredients list and method. Read through it once and you'll realise this recipe is actually very straightforward and requires very little hands-on cooking.

This is a great interactive sharing dish; stuff pieces of fish into the lettuce leaves (fresh corn tortillas would be great, too), top with the herbs and dipping sauce and let it trickle down your wrists as you eat with your hands. Tangerines and limes are used in both the butter and the dipping sauce; you'll need four tangerines and two limes in total.

————

Preheat the oven to 190°C fan/210°C.

Pat the sea bass with kitchen towel to make sure it's as dry as possible. Transfer it to a 33 x 26cm non-stick high-sided baking tray, arranging it diagonally, so it fits. The tray shouldn't be much bigger than the fish, otherwise the citrus butter will burn. Use a very sharp knife to make 5 diagonal slits in the fish. Season the cavity with ¼ teaspoon of fine salt, then stuff with the rosemary and spring onions.

Put all the ingredients for the citrus butter into a small saucepan and place on a medium heat just until the butter has melted. Pour over and around the fish.

Bake for 14 minutes (or longer if your fish is larger than 800g), then baste the fish well and turn the oven to the highest grill setting. Grill on the top shelf of the oven for 4–6 minutes, or until the skin begins to bubble and crisp. Keep a close eye, as some grills are much hotter than others.

While the fish is cooking, make the tangerine dipping sauce. Put the pul biber, garlic, ginger, tomato purée/paste and fine salt into a mortar and pound with a pestle to a rough paste.

Heat the oil in a small saucepan on a medium heat for 1 minute, then pour the hot oil into the mortar. Stir together, then add the chopped tomatoes, tangerine juice, lime juice and fish sauce.

Once cooked, transfer the sea bass to a large platter with the browned citrus butter. Discard the garlic skins and rosemary. Serve with the lettuce and fresh herbs to make parcels with, and the dipping sauce and lime wedges alongside.

MEAT

Spiced lamb and aubergine ragout

4 good-quality egg yolks

40g soy sauce

400g lamb mince

1 aubergine, cut into 2cm cubes (300g)

400g tin of chickpeas in salted
 water, drained and patted dry
 (240g drained weight)

200g sweet, ripe cherry tomatoes,
 finely chopped

2 limes: 1 tablespoon juice and the
 remainder cut into wedges

2 tablespoons olive oil

4 flatbreads, grilled

3 spring onions, julienned

5g fresh coriander leaves

Chipotle paste

2½ teaspoons chipotle chilli flakes

2 teaspoons ground cumin

2 large red chillies, deseeded
 and roughly chopped

100g tomato purée/paste

4 large cloves of garlic, roughly chopped

½ onion, roughly chopped

80g olive oil

2¼ teaspoons fine salt

Make ahead

The chipotle paste will keep in the fridge
for up to 2 weeks.

Notes

I strongly recommend doubling or tripling
the chipotle paste and keeping a stash
in the fridge. It's a flavour-packed umami
explosion that will lift soups, stews,
sauces and marinades to new heights.

The soy-cured yolk is completely optional
if you're out of eggs or you don't like the
idea of eating raw yolks, but is otherwise
highly recommended.

Lamb mince, chickpeas and aubergine cook together with chilli paste to create a simple one-tray ragout. I've suggested flatbreads to go with it, but the possibilities are endless. Serve it over pasta, rice or polenta, on grilled toast rubbed with garlic or with soft corn tortillas. Use it as the base for a pie, moussaka or lasagne. You can use beef or pork mince if you prefer, but you'll need to add more oil, as lamb mince is inherently fattier.

———

Preheat the oven to 220°C fan/240°C.

Carefully put the yolks, without breaking them, into a small bowl with the soy sauce and leave to cure while you cook the lamb, or for up to 2 hours (no longer, or they won't be oozy).

For the chipotle paste, put all the ingredients into a blender or small food processor and blitz to a smooth paste, scraping down the sides as needed.

Line a 38 x 29cm baking tray with parchment paper. Transfer three-quarters of the paste, along with the mince, aubergines and chickpeas, to the tray and mix well until thoroughly combined, breaking the mince apart as much as possible so it's not in chunks.

Bake for 25 minutes, or until the aubergines and chickpeas are crisp and golden-brown, stirring halfway through and breaking up any chunks of mince.

Meanwhile, in a small bowl, mix the remaining chipotle paste with the cherry tomatoes, lime juice and 2 tablespoons of oil to make a salsa.

Spoon the lamb and aubergine on to the warm flatbreads, then top with the tomato salsa, spring onions and coriander. Carefully top with the egg yolks (discard the soy marinade). Squeeze over the lime wedges and serve.

Chicken with pineapple and 'nduja

4 skin-on, bone-in chicken thighs,
    at room temperature

4 cloves of garlic, peeled and
    crushed with the side of a knife

1 medium onion, halved and very
    thinly sliced on a mandolin

½ large, extra-ripe pineapple,
    peeled (300g)

4 sweet tangerines (or 2 oranges),
    squeezed to get 100g juice (see notes)

100g chicken bone broth, stock or water

2 tablespoons double cream

5g fresh coriander

1 lime, cut into wedges

'Nduja and chipotle paste

50g 'nduja paste/spread

2 tablespoons olive oil

2 teaspoons tomato purée/paste

½ teaspoon chipotle flakes

½ teaspoon paprika

¾ teaspoon fine salt

about 20 twists of freshly ground
    black pepper

Get ahead

Marinate the chicken in the 'nduja and
chipotle paste up to 2 days ahead, but
don't mix in the onion and garlic until
you're ready to bake.

Notes

I use tangerines over oranges as they
have a more complex, floral flavour, but
feel free to use oranges if that's easier
(use fresh fruit, though, not juice from
a bottle or carton). If your tangerines/
oranges aren't particularly sweet, you may
want to add some maple syrup or honey –
do this when you add the stock or water.

I love the combination of sweet and savoury (as you'll probably have deduced if you've flicked through this book a few times), and there is no greater union than that of pork and pineapple. The pork here comes in the form of 'nduja, a spreadable chilli-spiked sausage from Calabria. Add chicken, pineapple, chipotle and tangerine to the mix and you've got yourself a party.

————

Preheat the oven to 180°C fan/200°C.

Put all the ingredients for the 'nduja and chipotle paste into a large bowl and mix together. Add the chicken, garlic and three-quarters of the sliced onion (save the rest to serve) and mix well so everything is coated evenly. Tip the chicken, onions and garlic into a 28cm ovenproof cast-iron skillet or similar-sized baking dish. Spread out the chicken thighs and arrange, skin side up, on top of the onions and garlic.

Cut the pineapple into 4 rounds, then cut each round into quarters, removing the hard core (you should have about 300g). Add the pineapple to the bowl with the remnants of the paste, mix to coat with whatever's left there, then arrange the pineapple around the chicken.

Pour the tangerine juice around the chicken (don't get the skin wet), then bake for 20 minutes. Remove from the oven and pour the stock or water into the pan around the chicken (again, don't get the skin wet). Return to the oven for another 20–25 minutes, or until the chicken is cooked through and the skin is browned and crispy. If you have a blowtorch, use it to char the pineapple a little.

Let the chicken rest for 5–10 minutes, then drizzle the cream into the sauce. Toss the coriander and the remaining sliced onions together with a tiny bit of oil and salt and arrange them on top. Serve from the pan, with the lime wedges alongside.

500g bavette steak, preferably cut into
    3 equal pieces weighing 160–170g each
300g ripe tomatoes
½ red onion
flaked salt
1 lemon, cut into wedges, to serve

Marinade

1 teaspoon fine salt
3 tablespoons olive oil
1 teaspoon Urfa chilli flakes
1½ teaspoons ground black lime (see notes)
about 50 twists of freshly ground
    black pepper

Soy and maple butter

40g ghee (from a jar not a tin, see page 17)
    or unsalted butter
1 tablespoon soy sauce or tamari
2½ teaspoons maple syrup
½ small clove of garlic, finely
    grated/crushed
¾ teaspoon ground black lime
¾ teaspoon Urfa chilli flakes

Notes

To grind black lime, crush 3 black limes
with the side of a knife to break them
open, then put into a blender and pulse
until finely ground. You won't need all
the lime for this recipe, but any less than
3 limes will be hard to grind in a blender.
Store any leftover lime in a sealed jar.

Get ahead

Marinate the steaks the day before and
keep refrigerated. Bring back to room
temperature before cooking.

Bavette resting over tomatoes with black lime and maple butter

Resting meat over perfectly ripe summer tomatoes is an easy way of creating something delicious, with the natural juices of the tomatoes and beef coming together with the black lime and maple butter to create something that you won't want to stop scarpetta-ing (*scarpetta* – the act of mopping up all the delicious juices/sauces on a plate with bread). You really want good-quality, ripe, sweet tomatoes for this. If tomatoes aren't in season, serve the bavette over peeled roasted peppers (use shop-bought or the recipe on page 149).

––––––––

If you have a large piece of bavette, first cut it down into portions weighing about 160g – that way they'll cook more evenly.

Pat the bavettes dry and transfer them to a large bowl. Add all the marinade ingredients and rub all over the steaks. Set aside to marinate for 10 minutes, or up to 1 hour.

Heat a large cast-iron skillet (or a large non-stick frying pan) on a high heat. Once very, very hot, place the bavettes in the pan, spaced apart, and sear for 2–4 minutes on each side (2 for rare, up to 4 for medium), pressing down with a spatula to get a dark-brown crust. Transfer to a board to rest for 8 minutes, flipping the steaks over halfway. Don't skip the resting part, it's crucial!

While the steaks are resting, slice the tomatoes and onions and arrange on a platter. Sprinkle over ½ teaspoon of flaked salt.

Melt the ghee in a small saucepan on a medium heat. Once melted and hot, remove from the heat and stir in the soy sauce, maple syrup, garlic, black lime and Urfa chilli flakes.

Slice the bavette against the grain and arrange over the tomatoes and onions. Sprinkle with flaked salt. Spoon over the soy and maple butter and serve with lemon wedges alongside.

300g fresh (or dried) pappardelle

extra virgin olive oil

Chipotle pancetta sauce

100g pancetta cubes (if your pancetta
is in a block, finely chop it before
adding it to the processor)

2¼ teaspoons chipotle flakes
(or less if you prefer milder heat)

½ teaspoon ground cumin

¼ teaspoon chilli flakes (optional)

100g tomato purée/paste

4 cloves of garlic, roughly chopped

¼ small onion, roughly chopped (20g)

75g olive oil, plus extra to serve

1½ teaspoons fine salt

about 50 twists of freshly ground
black pepper

Pappardelle with chipotle pancetta sauce

Only on very rare occasions will I hold back from covering a plate of pasta with Parmesan. Even when it comes to seafood pasta, I cannot and do not resist. This pasta sauce is so rich and complex that (and I can't quite believe I'm saying this) it doesn't need cheese. Of course, if you want to cover it in Parmesan or pecorino, you absolutely should. You can also cut the richness of the sauce by stirring in some finely chopped fresh cherry tomatoes or chopped parsley. FYI, the pancetta isn't meant to be crispy here, it's supposed to meld into the rich sauce.

―――――

Put all the ingredients for the chipotle pancetta sauce into a food processor or blender and pulse until you get a rough mash, scraping down the sides as you go. The onion and garlic should be broken down, but small pieces of pancetta are fine. If you don't have a food processor, finely grate or crush the garlic and very finely chop the onion until it almost resembles a mash before adding these to the remaining ingredients. Your sauce will be less smooth, as the pancetta cubes will be whole, but it will still be delicious.

Put the sauce into a cold sauté pan on a medium-high heat and cook, stirring often, for 5–6 minutes, until the sauce starts to bubble and spit. Turn the heat all the way down, then continue to cook, stirring often, for another 3 minutes. Set the pan aside.

Cook your pasta in well-salted boiling water until al dente, then drain, reserving 325g of the pasta water.

Return the sauté pan of sauce to a medium heat, then add the drained pasta and the pasta water. Cook for 2 minutes, tossing the pan until the pasta water and the sauce emulsify.

Remove from the heat and serve at once, drizzled with extra virgin olive oil.

Notes

The sauce will keep for up to a week
in the fridge.

300g carrots, peeled and cut
      into 2cm chunks

1 red onion, cut into sixths

5 cloves of garlic, peeled

2 large mild red chillies, halved
      lengthways (optional)

3 tablespoons olive oil

1½ teaspoons maple syrup

½ teaspoon chipotle flakes

1 teaspoon red bell pepper flakes
      (or ½ teaspoon Aleppo chilli/pul biber)

1 teaspoon ground cumin

¾ teaspoon fine salt

8 good-quality, fatty sausages
      (preferably Tuscan or Sicilian style)

90g water

1 lime, halved

1 tangerine, halved

1 lemon, halved

200g salted jarred or tinned beans/
      chickpeas, drained (optional)

Cucumber salsa

½ cucumber, peeled, halved and
      watery centre scraped out

1 tablespoon lime juice

2 teaspoons olive oil

⅛ teaspoon fine salt

5g fresh coriander, finely chopped

5g fresh chives, finely chopped

Sausage and charred citrus traybake

Lemon, lime and tangerine all in the same recipe might seem like overkill, but trust me on this, each one brings its own distinctive character to the party. What you'll end up with, once the charred citrus juices have been added to the roasting juices, is a wonderfully aromatic sweet and sour sauce. Stir some tinned or jarred beans into the sauce to make it a bulkier meal, or serve with grilled bread to mop up all the juices. It's important to use good-quality, fatty sausages, as you want their delicious juices to run into the veg and sauce and not dry out. If you can find Tuscan or Sicilian fennel and chilli sausages, you know you're on to something good.

———

Preheat the oven to 200°C fan/220°C.

Place the first 12 ingredients (everything from the carrots to the sausages) in a large, 34 x 28cm, high-sided baking tray. Mix very well, then spread the sausages out. Pour the water into the tray around the sausages (don't get them wet!).

Roast for 35–40 minutes, turning the vegetables (but not the sausages) a couple of times, until the sausages are cooked through and the vegetables are golden-brown.

While the tray is in the oven, place a large, non-stick frying pan on a high heat. Once very hot, place the citrus halves cut side down in the pan and char for 3½–4 minutes, or until the cut sides are nicely charred (press down on the citrus to make sure they colour evenly).

For the salsa, chop the cucumber into 1cm cubes. Mix the cucumber together with lime juice, oil and fine salt. Just before serving, stir in the herbs.

Transfer the contents of the baking tray to a platter or serve from the tray. Squeeze over the charred citrus, then stir in the beans (if using). Top with some of the cucumber salsa, serving the rest on the side.

TERRING

(KIND OF)

ING

First things first. When I talk about **ENTERTAINING**, I'm not talking about the kind of entertaining that involves aprons and fluffed-up cushions, I'm literally talking about entertaining in the truest sense of the word: 'providing amusement or enjoyment'.

The recipes in this chapter will take a little longer, so they're for when you're in a certain frame of mind. Maybe you have some time on your hands and are in the mood to cook something a little more challenging. Perhaps you have friends coming over and you want to pull out all the stops.

Whether you're cooking for friends, partners, flatmates or for yourself is less important – it's about the enjoyment of the process as well as the result. These are the recipes to experiment with when you want to slow down and really savour that process. These are the recipes to take your time over, for the love of cooking. The act of chopping ingredients finely and cooking them slowly might be a meditative experience for you. I respect that. I hope you'll feel right at home here.

There are countless dishes in this section that could naturally take centre stage at a dinner party (see Chard rotolo, page 161, or Celebration salmon, page 192), but that's not to say that these recipes are only for those occasions. You could just as easily make the Celebration salmon for yourself, freeze half and have leftovers for days. In fact, I very much encourage this by suggesting how to turn the leftovers into fried rice (page 193).

Roast chicken curry with crispy curry leaves (page 222) is another great example of a recipe that's special enough to be a centrepiece for a crowd, but can also be made just for you, with leftovers. See Cannelloni enchiladas (page 225), where I suggest you use your leftover roast chicken to make a whole new, exciting meal.

And of course, if you're not in the mood for longer recipes, you can always flip back to **EVERYDAY** (page 20) for quicker, more straightforward meals.

VEG

Sticky coconut rice cake with turmeric tomatoes

Turmeric tomatoes

400g sweet, ripe cherry tomatoes,
    such as Datterini

15g fresh ginger, peeled and julienned

15g fresh coriander, stalks and leaves

3 cloves of garlic, peeled

70g olive oil

2 teaspoons maple syrup or honey

½ teaspoon ground turmeric

1¼ teaspoons cumin seeds

½ teaspoon fine salt

Rice cake

400g Thai sticky rice (aka glutinous
    rice or sweet rice), soaked for 1 hour
    in plenty of water, then drained
    (see notes)

400g tin of full-fat coconut milk
    (at least 70% coconut extract)

250g water

2 small cloves of garlic, finely
    grated/crushed

2 teaspoons finely grated fresh ginger

2 spring onions, very finely chopped (25g)

1½ teaspoons fine salt

To serve

2 spring onions, finely sliced

5g fresh coriander

1 lime, cut into wedges

Notes

I use the Thai Taste brand of sticky rice,
which only needs to soak for 1 hour in order
for it to cook through. If you're using another
brand, check the side of the packet, as it
may need to be soaked overnight.

Make ahead

Both parts of the dish can be made the day
before and reheated in a warm oven .

This recipe is almost completely hands off and requires very little prep.
Make sure you start by soaking the rice, then all you have to do is crush garlic,
julienne ginger and chop spring onions. Both the rice cake and the tomatoes
bake in the oven at the same time and don't need to be stirred or basted, leaving
you to get on with other things. Leftover rice cake slices are great pan-fried
the next day, in a little oil, until crispy.

This dish is vegan as it is, but I love it with crispy fried eggs, too. The sticky rice
cake, without the tomatoes, is a great side to the Celebration salmon (page
192), the Roast chicken curry (page 222) and the Mussels and orzo in a coconut
and saffron stew (page 99).

———————

Preheat the oven to 230°C fan/250°C. Line a 23 x 23cm baking tin (or a
similar-sized ovenproof dish) with non-stick parchment paper.

For the tomatoes, put all the ingredients into an ovenproof dish that's just
big enough for them all to fit snugly in a single layer.

Whisk all the ingredients for the rice cake together, making sure to get rid of any
lumps of coconut milk. Pour into the prepared tin and flatten the top. The liquid
should just cover the surface of the rice. If it doesn't, you need a smaller tin/dish.

Put both dishes in the oven – the tomatoes on the top shelf and the rice on
the shelf below (or preferably both on the top shelf, if they'll fit). Bake for
30 minutes. The tomatoes should be soft and slightly charred and the rice
should be cooked through and golden-brown on top.

Remove both dishes from the oven. Cover the tomatoes to keep them warm.
Leave the rice to rest for 20 minutes. Turn the oven grill to its highest setting.

After 20 minutes, lift the rice cake on to a flat baking tray with the paper.
Tear away any overhanging parchment that could burn under the grill. Grill for
5–8 minutes near the top of the oven, or until the rice is crisp and golden-brown
on top. All grills are different so this could take more or less time. If you have a
blowtorch, use it to crisp up and lightly char the surface a little more.

Leave to cool for 5 minutes before slicing into squares. Serve with the warm
tomatoes and garnish with the spring onions, coriander and lime wedges.

1kg cassava (1–3 roots, depending on size)

900g sunflower oil, for frying

flaked salt, to serve

2 limes, cut into wedges, to serve

Lime mayo

50g Kewpie mayonnaise (or another mayo)

50g crème fraîche

1 teaspoon finely grated lime zest

Chilli butter

60g ghee (from a jar not a tin, see page 17)
    or unsalted butter

1 clove of garlic, very finely chopped

1 tablespoon hot sauce (I use Kold Sauce
    but you can use Tabasco or Encona)

½ teaspoon smoked paprika

⅛ teaspoon fine salt

Macaxeira frita with chilli butter and lime mayo

In Brazil, the root most commonly known around the world as cassava goes by many other names – *aipim*, *yuca*, *mandioca*, *macaxeira* – depending on where you're from. My mum is from Natal in the north-east of Brazil, where it's called *macaxeira*, and where I first fell in love with this fluffy-on-the-inside, crispy-on-the-outside preparation for this most versatile of roots. Similarly to potato, *macaxeira* can be fried, boiled or roasted, or it can be processed into flour or starch to be used as a bulker, binder or a thickener. In this instance it's boiled, fried, then tossed in clarified butter, or, as we call it in Brazil, *manteiga de garrafa*, which roughly translates as 'bottle butter', so called because of its liquid state.

If you can't get hold of cassava, you can use golden sweet potatoes, or regular potatoes instead.

———————

Mix together all the ingredients for the lime mayo. Set aside.

For the chilli butter, put all the ingredients into a small saucepan and place on a low heat. Gently cook for 2 minutes, then remove from the heat and set aside in the pan to infuse.

Use a very sharp peeler or knife to peel the cassava roots, removing the thick brown skin as well as the layer of pink flesh beneath it. Discard any pieces of cassava that are soft or blackened. Cut the cassava into roughly 6 x 2cm batons – you'll need a sharp knife for this too.

Bring a large pot of well-salted water to the boil on a high heat. Once boiling, lower the heat to medium. Boil the cassava pieces for about 14 minutes, or until they are very soft and fluffy but still holding their shape. Drain well and transfer to a tray lined with absorbent kitchen towel. Some pieces of cassava will have a hard, fibrous inner root running through them, which is easily removed once the cassava is cool enough to handle.

Continues on next page...

Make ahead

The lime mayo will keep for up to 3 weeks in the fridge.

Macaxiera frita continued...

Heat the frying oil in a large sauté pan or wok on a medium heat. Place a colander on a tray. Test the oil is hot enough by dropping in a small piece of cassava. Once it starts to sizzle, you're ready to start frying. If you have a temperature probe, the oil should be at 180°C.

Carefully add the cassava to the oil and fry until golden-brown and crisp all over, about 8 minutes, turning frequently. If you only have a small or medium pan, fry it in batches. Transfer the fries to the colander for the oil to drain away. Sprinkle with flaked salt and toss well.

Return the chilli butter to a medium heat until warm and melted.

Transfer the chips to a platter and pour over the chilli butter. Serve with the lime mayo alongside, and plenty of lime juice squeezed on top.

Butternut and sage lasagne gratin

½ large butternut squash, peeled and
    seeds scooped out (500g)

400g sweet, ripe cherry tomatoes,
    such as Datterini, halved

4 cloves of garlic, finely grated/crushed

1 tablespoon tomato purée/paste

2¾ teaspoons fine salt

5g fresh sage leaves, roughly chopped,
    plus 10 extra leaves to serve

6 tablespoons olive oil, plus extra to finish

220g double cream, plus 2 tablespoons
    to serve

80g Parmesan, finely grated,
    plus extra to serve

¾ teaspoon freshly grated nutmeg

250–300g dried lasagne sheets

400g chicken stock (or veg stock/water)

freshly ground black pepper

flaked salt

This lasagne is covered with stock and cooked rather like you would a gratin, which means you can layer the dried pasta with raw butternut slices, without having to pre-roast them. What's more, there's no béchamel, so it all comes together quickly. I've kept this recipe very simple, but spinach, chard leaves and ham are all great additions to the layers.

I like to use chicken stock or bone broth here, but you could use veg stock or water to keep it vegetarian, and plant-based cream and cheese to keep it vegan.

————

Preheat the oven to 220°C fan/240°C.

Using a mandolin or a sharp knife, very thinly slice the butternut into 4mm-thick half moons.

In a large bowl, mix together the butternut, halved tomatoes, garlic, tomato purée/paste, fine salt, chopped sage, 4 tablespoons of oil and plenty of pepper (this is easiest with your hands). Set aside.

In a separate bowl, mix the cream, Parmesan and nutmeg together. Set 80g of this mixture aside to use later.

Cover the bottom of a 28 x 23cm baking dish with a layer of lasagne sheets, then follow with a layer of the butternut mixture, spread out. Spoon over some of the cream mixture, then continue layering in the same way until you've run out of pasta, butternut and cream. Pour the stock/water evenly over, then cover tightly with foil and bake for 50 minutes.

Remove from the oven and discard the foil. Spoon over the reserved 80g of cream mixture and return the dish, uncovered, to the oven for 10 minutes.

In a small bowl, mix the remaining 2 tablespoons of oil with the remaining 10 sage leaves. Spoon the leaves and oil over the lasagne and return it to the oven for a final 5–6 minutes, or until the sage leaves are bright green and crisp, and the lasagne is golden-brown.

Leave to rest for 10 minutes, then finish with the 2 tablespoons of cream, a good drizzle of oil and plenty of grated Parmesan, flaked salt and black pepper.

Make ahead

Assemble up to a day ahead. Keep
in the fridge and bring back to room
temperature before baking.

6 large eggs

2 tablespoons milk or water

1 tablespoon olive oil, plus extra for frying

¼ teaspoon fine salt

Charred red pepper sauce

3 red romano peppers (300g)

1 small clove of garlic, finely
    grated/crushed

130g double cream

2 tablespoons olive oil

1 lemon: 1½ teaspoons finely grated
    zest and ½ tablespoon juice

50g Parmesan, finely grated,
    plus extra to serve

¼ teaspoon freshly grated nutmeg

1 teaspoon tomato purée/paste (or
    red pepper paste if you can find it)

⅓ teaspoon fine salt

about 50 twists of freshly ground
    black pepper

Notes

You'll need a non-stick frying pan to
make the noodles. My large frying pan
is 30cm wide. If yours is smaller, you'll
need to fry more omelettes to ensure
they're as thin as crêpes.

Make ahead

The charred red pepper sauce will keep
in the fridge for up to 3 days – just leave
out the lemon juice and add it just before
you heat up the sauce.

Charred red pepper sauce with omelette noodles

I've called this recipe 'Charred red pepper sauce with omelette noodles' rather than 'Omelette noodles with charred red pepper sauce' because you can absolutely serve the sauce with shop-bought or homemade pasta if you prefer (gnocchi would be great, too). Having said that, the omelette noodles are a great experiment for anyone who is gluten intolerant, on a grain-free diet, or who, like me, simply loves eggs in all shapes and forms.

This recipe serves 2 because, although the noodles aren't hard to make, they do involve frying 4 (or more, if your pan is small) omelettes. If you have the time and want to make these for a group, double the noodle and sauce recipes.

———————

Preheat the oven to the highest grill setting.

Arrange the peppers on a rack set over a baking tray. Grill on the top shelf of the oven until soft and blackened in patches, about 7–8 minutes, then turn the peppers and grill for another 4–8 minutes, or until that side is soft and blackened in patches too. Keep an eye on them – they may be ready sooner if your grill runs hot. Set aside and leave to cool.

Put all the ingredients for the noodles into a medium bowl and whisk until fully combined. Pour into a measuring jug.

Heat a large (30cm) non-stick frying pan (see notes) on a medium-high heat. Once hot, grease the pan with 1 teaspoon of oil and turn the heat down to medium-low. Pour a quarter (or less, if your pan is small) of the egg mixture into the pan and immediately swirl the pan so the egg covers the surface evenly – it should be about as thin as a crêpe. Cook for about 1 minute 15 seconds, or until the top of the omelette is no longer wet or sticky. Remove the pan from the heat and use a spatula to help you roll up the omelette, then slide the roll on to a chopping board (see pictures on next page). Continue in the same way with the remaining mixture, until you have four long rolls.

Remove the stalks and seeds from the peppers, then transfer the peppers (including the skin and any liquid) to a blender. Add all the remaining sauce ingredients and blitz until smooth.

Continues on next page...

Omelette noodles continued...

Line up the omelette rolls. With a sharp knife, slice them widthways at 2cm intervals. Use your hands to carefully separate and unravel the noodles.

Return the frying pan to a medium heat with the sauce. Warm for 1–2 minutes, then remove from the heat and add the noodles. Carefully toss so the noodles are coated in sauce, being careful not to break them, then transfer to plates. Finish with plenty of Parmesan, oil and black pepper.

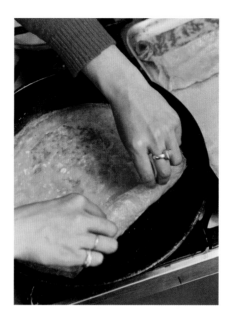

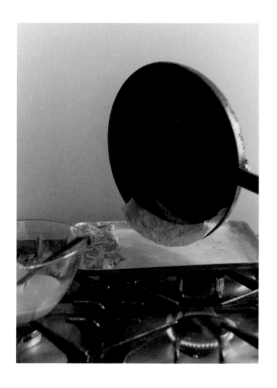

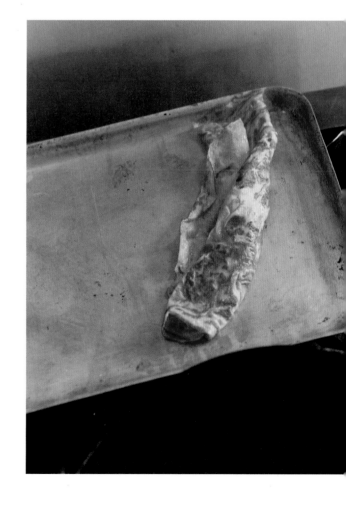

Crunchy spelt chipotle pastry

90g unsalted butter in one piece, frozen

120g wholemeal/dark spelt flour,
    plus extra for dusting (or regular
    wholemeal flour)

40g quick-cook polenta

2½ teaspoons soft light brown
    sugar or caster sugar

½ teaspoon fine salt

about 10 twists of freshly ground
    black pepper

½ teaspoon chipotle flakes

20g olive oil

70g ice-cold water

1 egg, whisked, for brushing the pastry

Ricotta yoghurt

80g full-fat ricotta

80g Greek-style yoghurt

½ small clove of garlic, finely
    grated/crushed

½ teaspoon finely grated lime zest

¼ teaspoon ground cumin

5g fresh chives, finely chopped

⅛ teaspoon fine salt

Marinated tomatoes

600g ripe tomatoes (preferably
    a mix of colours and sizes,
    including cherry tomatoes)

1 banana shallot, thinly sliced into rounds

1½ teaspoons soft light brown sugar

2 tablespoons olive oil

1 jalapeño, finely chopped (optional)

1–2 limes: ½ teaspoon finely grated zest
    and 1½ tablespoons juice

½ teaspoon fine salt

½ teaspoon ground cumin

To serve

5g fresh basil

2 spring onions, julienned (15g)

1 jalapeño, thinly sliced into
    rounds (optional)

¼ teaspoon chipotle flakes

Tomato and lime galette with crunchy spelt chipotle pastry

My top tip for this recipe would be to make the pastry the day before, or at least a few hours ahead. Pastry making is unavoidably messy (or at least it is for me), so breaking the recipe down into bite-size chunks is a great way of giving yourself time to nail the pastry, clean down floury surfaces and breeze through the other (incredibly easy) elements of the galette in a clean kitchen. You can prepare the pastry up until the point when it's rolled out the day before – just cover it with cling film before you refrigerate it if you're leaving it overnight. Don't prep the ricotta yoghurt or marinated tomatoes until you're ready to bake.

———

First, make sure you freeze your block of butter for at least 30 minutes.

Put the flour, polenta, sugar, salt, pepper and chipotle flakes into a large bowl and stir to combine. Remove the butter from the freezer and grate, using the large holes of a box grater (or chop into small pieces). Add to the bowl along with the oil and water. Bring together into a ball, but don't overwork the dough – you want visible pieces of butter throughout.

Dust your work surface with flour, then tip the pastry ball out on to it. Roll the pastry out into an A4-size rectangle, flouring the pin, pastry and surface as needed so the pastry doesn't stick.

Fold the shorter ends of the pastry to meet in the middle, roll out, then fold the longer sides in to meet in the middle and roll out again. Fold the pastry in half, roll out once more, then shape into a smooth round disc, approximately 12cm-wide. Cover tightly with cling film and freeze for 30 minutes. If you're getting ahead with the pastry and making it more than 30 minutes ahead, keep it in the fridge.

Flour your surface once more and roll the pastry out into a rough 30cm-wide circle/oval. Transfer it to a large, parchment-lined baking tray that will fit into your fridge, then refrigerate for 30 minutes.

Preheat the oven to 200°C fan/220°C.

Mix all the ingredients for the ricotta yoghurt together in a medium bowl. Cut the tomatoes into random bite-size pieces and place in a separate bowl with all the remaining ingredients for the marinated tomatoes. Gently mix together.

Continues on next page...

Tomato galette continued...

Remove the tray from the fridge and spread the ricotta yoghurt mixture over the pastry, leaving a 4cm rim around the edge. Top the ricotta yoghurt with half the marinated tomatoes, avoiding the liquid and leaving the 4cm rim uncovered.

Fold the edges of the pastry up and over the edges of the tomatoes. Brush the exposed pastry with egg, then bake for 30 minutes, rotating the tray halfway. Leave to cool for 10 minutes.

Arrange the rest of the fresh tomatoes on top of the roasted tomatoes. Drizzle over a couple of teaspoons of the tomato marinade. Top with the basil, spring onions, jalapeño and chipotle flakes. Finish with extra virgin olive oil, flaked salt and black pepper, and serve.

Make ahead

Unrolled, the pastry will keep in the fridge for up to 3 days, just make sure it's covered tightly with cling film.

4 large eggs (optional)

5g fresh parsley, finely chopped

5g fresh chives, finely chopped

½ lemon

freshly ground black pepper

Aïoli

3 onions, skin left on and quartered

75g olive oil

¼ teaspoon fine salt

1 whole garlic bulb

2 teaspoons lemon juice

2 teaspoons English mustard

3 tablespoons double cream

    (or vegan alternative)

Beans

450g cooked beans (drained weight)

(preferably jarred but tinned is fine too,

see intro)

120g chicken stock (or veg stock/water)

1 tablespoon lemon juice, plus 1 lemon

    cut into wedges, to serve

¼ teaspoon fine salt

Make ahead

The aïoli will keep in the fridge for up

to 2 weeks.

Notes

You can use any tinned bean, pulse

or lentil here – just make sure they're

kept in salted water, because it's almost

impossible to penetrate an unsalted,

tinned bean with flavour.

Beans with roasted onion aïoli

This dish is all about the aïoli – which isn't technically an aïoli at all, because it features cream instead of yolks and is made with roasted onions and garlic. In this context, it completely jazzes up tinned beans. It will do similar such things to just about anything you pair it with: crudités, crisps, grilled asparagus, sausages, sandwiches – it's that good. The soft-boiled eggs are optional – you can leave them out and use a plant-based cream to keep the dish vegan.

Use any bean you like here. I prefer jarred beans because they're soft and perfectly seasoned. If using tinned, you'll need 2 x 400g tins – make sure they're in salted water.

———————

Preheat the oven to 220°C fan/240°C.

Start with the aïoli. Place the onions in a baking dish, drizzle with 1 tablespoon of oil and sprinkle with ¼ teaspoon of fine salt. Toss so the onions are covered in oil, then arrange so that one of the cut sides of each quarter is facing down.

Cut the top off the garlic bulb to expose the cloves, then wrap the bulb in foil and place in the baking dish.

Roast for 18 minutes, then lower the heat to 180°C fan/200°C and roast for another 12 minutes, or until the onions are soft and golden brown. Remove the onion and garlic from the tray and set aside until completely cool.

Meanwhile, if using the eggs, pour boiling water into a small saucepan and place on a medium heat. Once at a rolling boil, turn the heat down and carefully add the eggs. Cook for 6½ minutes, then immediately transfer the eggs to a bowl of cold water, letting the cold tap run over the bowl for a few minutes. Gently bash the eggs on a hard surface, so the shell is shattered all over. Peel the eggs under running water, then set the peeled eggs aside.

Put all the ingredients for the beans into a medium saucepan. Add more salt to taste, if needed. Bring to a simmer over a medium heat and cook for 3 minutes, until warmed through. Set aside.

Once cool, remove the skin from the onions, as well as the dry layer beneath it. Set aside 4 onion quarters to be used later.

Continues on next page...

Beans with roasted onion aïoli continued...

Put the remaining onions (8 quarters) into a small food processor. Unwrap the garlic bulb, then squeeze the soft cloves into the processor, discarding the skin.

Add the remaining 60g of oil, the lemon juice, mustard, double cream and ¾ teaspoon of fine salt. Blitz until smooth, scraping down the sides as you go. If you don't have a food processor, very finely chop the onion and garlic and stir together with the remaining aïoli ingredients. It won't have the texture of aïoli, but it will still be delicious.

Spread the aioli out on a lipped platter, then top with the beans. Top with the onion petals. Halve the eggs (if using) and arrange on the platter. Sprinkle over the herbs, then finish with a good drizzle of olive oil, some black pepper and flaked salt. Squeeze over some lemon juice and serve with grilled bread.

Makes 8 quesadillas

60g feta, crumbled into small pieces

80g Gruyère, finely grated

120g mozzarella, drained and torn
into small pieces

1 tablespoon chives, finely chopped

1 tablespoon ghee (from a jar not a tin,
see page 17) or unsalted butter

1 tablespoon olive oil

runny honey, to serve (optional)

2 limes, cut into wedges

Tortillas (makes 8 x 12cm tortillas)

90g masa harina (I use Bob's Red Mill)

50g fine, quick-cook polenta
(I use Valsugana, see notes)

40g ghee or unsalted butter, softened

½ teaspoon ground cumin

⅓ teaspoon fine salt

180g boiling water

Habanero oil

100g olive oil

2 teaspoons tomato purée/paste

1 teaspoon chipotle flakes

1 dried habanero, seeds discarded, finely
chopped (use less habanero or a pinch
of regular chilli flakes if you prefer)

½ teaspoon sweet paprika

¼ teaspoon fine salt

Make ahead

Fill the tortillas with the cheese mixture
the day before and keep covered
and refrigerated. Bring back to room
temperature before frying.

Notes

You need the fine, quick-cook variety
of polenta for this; look at the packet and
as long as the cooking time is 8 minutes
or less, you're good to go. Coarse polenta
that takes 40 minutes plus to cook won't
work and will result in a dry, crunchy dough.

Three cheese quesadillas with habanero oil

This is not a traditional tortilla recipe (I am no expert and there are plenty of resources for traditional recipes). Having said that, I am very happy with this version of tortillas, which I've tweaked more times than I can count before landing here. They contain polenta, ghee and cumin as well as masa harina and water; the polenta gives the tortillas an extra dimension of 'corniness' and a subtle crunch, and the ghee adds richness, which is something I enjoy in traditional wheat flour tortillas that contain lard.

_____

For the tortillas, put the masa harina, polenta, ghee, cumin and salt into a large bowl. Slowly pour in the boiling water, stirring as you go, until the water and ghee are fully incorporated. Form the mixture into a smooth mass – the dough will be a little wet and sticky at this point, but the water will absorb as it rests. Cover the dough with a clean, damp tea towel and leave to rest for 20 minutes.

While the dough is resting, put all the ingredients for the habanero oil into a small saucepan and whisk well to incorporate the tomato purée/paste. Place on a medium heat and cook until gently bubbling, about 1½ minutes. Remove from the heat and set aside.

Cut out six 16cm discs of non-stick parchment paper. Heat a large frying pan on a high heat.

Lightly dampen your tea towel again. Divide the dough into 8 portions weighing about 40g each and keep covered with the damp tea towel. With slightly damp hands, roll each portion in the palm of your hands into a smooth ball and, once formed, store under the damp tea towel.

Prepare your work surface with a tortilla press, the parchment paper discs and another slightly damp tea towel. If you don't have a tortilla press, use a heavy-bottomed pan.

Once the frying pan is very hot, you're ready to go. Keeping the rest covered with the damp cloth, roll one of the balls of dough in the palm of your hands to get rid of any surface cracks and to make sure it's smooth.

Continues on next page...

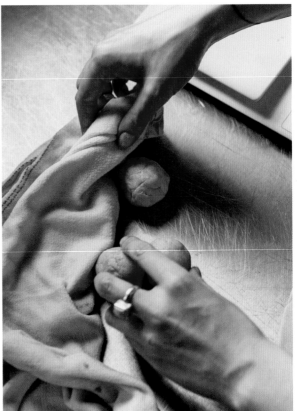

Three cheese quesadillas continued...

Use the tortilla press (or heavy-bottomed pan) to press the dough ball between two discs of paper into a 12cm-wide tortilla. Remove the top sheet of paper and use the bottom sheet to help you transfer the tortilla to the hot pan.

Once in the pan, carefully peel away the paper. Cook the tortilla for 1½ minutes on the first side, then flip and cook for another 1 minute on the other side. Once cooked, wrap the tortilla in the slightly damp tea towel.

Continue with the rest of the dough balls in the same way, cooking as many tortillas as you can fit into the pan as you gain confidence. You'll probably need to turn the heat down to medium or medium-low after you've cooked a couple of tortillas, so they don't burn or get too dry. Keep the tortillas wrapped in the tea towel.

Mix all three cheeses together in a medium bowl with the chives. Once cool enough to handle, add 30g of the cheese to one half of each tortilla, then fold into a half moon and set aside. Don't worry if some of them crack along the straight edge, this leads to cheese spilling out, which leads to crispy cheese, which is no bad thing.

Preheat the oven to 150°C fan/170°C.

Once all the tortillas have been filled, return the pan to a high heat with ½ tablespoon of ghee and ½ tablespoon of oil. Once the ghee is melted and hot, cook the quesadillas 4 at a time (if they'll fit) for 1½–2 minutes on each side (they should sizzle as soon as they hit the pan), or until the cheese has melted and the quesadillas are golden-brown. Transfer to a tray and keep warm in the oven while you fry the rest with the remaining ghee and oil.

Transfer to a platter and spoon over some of the habanero oil. Drizzle over a little honey, if you like the combination of sweet and savoury. Serve with the lime wedges squeezed on top.

Sweet and sour celery salad

60g golden (or regular) raisins

1 medium celery bunch, with the leaves

1 tablespoon olive oil

¼ teaspoon fine salt

25g pine nuts

5g fresh basil leaves

1 tablespoon fresh chives, finely chopped

¼ teaspoon Urfa chilli flakes

¼ teaspoon pul biber (or use
    Aleppo chilli/red pepper flakes)

125g ricotta (optional)

Dressing

2½ tablespoons soy sauce or tamari

2 tablespoons lemon juice

2 tablespoons olive oil

1 tablespoon maple syrup or honey

1 clove of garlic, very finely chopped

about 8 twists of freshly ground
    black pepper

If you're thinking of giving this salad a miss, think again, because this unassuming dish was actually one of the team's favourite recipes when we shot the book. Cooked celery is highly underrated, and the celery here is lightly charred and slightly soft, which helps it soak up the delicious sweet and sour dressing. The ricotta is completely optional and the salad is still wonderful without it; leave it out to keep the salad vegan, or use a plant-based cheese alternative if you can get a good one.

———

Put the raisins into a bowl and cover with boiling water. Leave to soak while you char the celery.

Remove the leaves of the celery. Set aside 10g of the brightest leaves in a small bowl. Cut 400g of the stalks at an angle into 4cm-long pieces (cut any of the wider stalks in half lengthways first). Toss the celery stalk pieces together with the oil and fine salt. Use any remaining celery in another recipe.

Place a large frying pan on a medium-high heat. Toast the pine nuts for 2½–3 minutes, tossing a few times, until nicely browned. Transfer them to a plate. Add the celery to the pan, increase the heat to high, and cook for 4 minutes undisturbed. Toss the celery and cook for another 5–6 minutes undisturbed, or until it is nicely charred in places. Take the pan off the heat and cover it with a plate or lid, so the celery softens a little in the residual heat.

Mix all the dressing ingredients together in a large bowl. Drain the raisins, then finely chop them and add them to the dressing. Stir in the cooked celery and leave for 5–10 minutes.

Stir in half each of the celery leaves, basil and chives. Transfer the celery and dressing to a lipped platter and sprinkle over the Urfa and pul biber. Spoon over the ricotta, if using, and finish with the remaining celery leaves, basil, chives and the pine nuts.

5 red romano peppers (500g)

⅛ teaspoon fine salt

tahini, to serve

good-quality crisps, to serve (plain,
    salt & pepper, or salt & vinegar)

Ginger dressing

50g fresh ginger, peeled and julienned

⅛ teaspoon fine salt

4 tablespoons olive oil

1 small clove of garlic, finely
    grated/crushed

2 tablespoons soy sauce or tamari (use
    a bit less if adding Chinkiang vinegar)

2 tablespoons freshly squeezed
    tangerine juice

½ tablespoon maple syrup or honey

½ teaspoon Chinkiang vinegar (optional,
    if you have some)

¼ teaspoon Urfa chilli

Charred red pepper tartare with crispy ginger dressing

This is a great dip for sharing, but would also make a lovely individually plated starter if you're feeling fancy. Roasted aubergine cubes are a delicious addition to the peppers, and of course if you don't need this to be vegan, you can treat it like a traditional tartare and swap the charred peppers for raw beef or tuna (in which case you won't need to turn the oven on).

———

Preheat the oven to the highest grill setting. Arrange the peppers on a rack set over a baking tray. Grill until soft and blackened in patches, about 7 minutes, then turn the peppers and grill for another 4–8 minutes, until that side is soft and blackened in patches too. Keep an eye on them – they may be ready sooner if your grill runs hot. Transfer to a bowl and cover with a plate while you fry the ginger.

Prepare a metal sieve set over a medium heatproof bowl. Toss the ginger with ⅛ teaspoon of fine salt.

Put the olive oil into a medium saucepan on a medium-low heat with one piece of the ginger. Once the ginger starts to sizzle, add the rest of it to the oil and gently fry, stirring often with a fork to separate the pieces, until the ginger is crisp and light golden. This should take about 3½ minutes, but keep a close eye on it as it can turn from golden to brown and burnt quite quickly. Strain the crispy ginger through the sieve, collecting the oil. Set the crispy ginger aside on a plate.

Add the garlic, soy sauce, tangerine juice, maple syrup, Chinkiang vinegar (if using) and Urfa chilli to the bowl of oil.

Peel the peppers and remove the seeds and stalks. Chop the flesh into 1cm squares, season with ⅛ teaspoon fine salt, then add to the bowl. Stir together, then leave to marinate for 10 minutes, or overnight.

To plate like the picture, strain the peppers over a bowl to collect the marinade and leave to drain for a minute. Transfer the peppers to a bowl and pat them down, then tip the bowl on to a platter. Lift off the bowl, then make a well in the centre of the peppers with the back of a spoon, and fill the well with tahini. Spoon the marinade over the peppers (but not over the tahini). Top with the crispy ginger and serve with crisps on the side for dipping.

Make ahead

You can roast and marinate the peppers up to 2 days ahead – however, the ginger will only stay crispy for a day.

Brown butter curried cornbread

140g unsalted butter, plus extra to serve

500g frozen corn kernels, defrosted
    and patted dry

150g Greek-style yoghurt

2 large eggs

1 Scotch bonnet chilli, finely chopped
    (optional, see notes)

1 spring onion, finely chopped

5g fresh ginger, peeled and finely grated

1½ teaspoons medium curry powder

1½ teaspoons finely grated lime zest

100g fine, quick-cook polenta (see notes)

80g plain flour

½ teaspoon fine salt

6 tablespoons maple syrup, plus extra
    to serve

½ teaspoon baking powder

½ teaspoon bicarbonate of soda

flaked salt, to serve

Cornbread is usually a supporting act, but this version is good enough to take centre stage at the dinner table and will probably end up being the dish around which you plan the meal. The corn that bejewels the surface is best just out of the oven when it's a little crispy from the butter, and a little sticky from the maple syrup. That's not to say you need to eat it all in one go; it will still be delicious the next day, heated up. To heat, either pan-fry, or place the slices on a tray in a cold oven, turn the temperature up to 150°C fan/170°C and warm for about 10 minutes. Serve with plenty of butter on the side.

This cornbread goes really well with the Roast chicken curry (page 222) and the Mole short ribs (page 227).

———

Preheat the oven to 200°C fan/220°C. Line and grease a 20cm cake tin.

Melt the butter in a medium saucepan over a medium heat for 5–6 minutes, stirring often until the butter foams and then turns a deep golden-brown. Add the corn and leave to bubble away for 4 minutes, stirring every so often. Remove from the heat and set aside to cool for 10 minutes.

While the corn and butter mixture is cooling, put the yoghurt, eggs, Scotch bonnet, spring onion, ginger, curry powder, lime zest, polenta, flour, salt and 3 tablespoons of maple syrup into a food processor, but don't blitz yet.

Once cool, set aside 140g of the corn and butter mixture in a small bowl to use later. Add the remaining corn and butter to the food processor, then add the baking powder and bicarbonate of soda. Pulse about 3–5 times, just until the mixture comes together. Don't overmix, you want a textured batter with small chunks of corn, not a smooth batter.

Transfer the batter into the prepared tin, then spoon the reserved corn and butter evenly over the surface.

Bake for 20 minutes, then evenly drizzle over the remaining 3 tablespoons of maple syrup and bake for another 15–20 minutes, or until crisp and golden brown on top.

Leave to cool for 15 minutes before releasing from the tin. If you have a blowtorch, use it to char the corn in places. Drizzle over some more maple syrup (I like a lot!), sprinkle with flaked salt and serve with a slab of butter alongside.

Notes

I use a whole Scotch bonnet, and its flavour and heat is quite dominant. I love that, but you can of course add less, removing the pith and seeds, or just add a pinch of regular chilli flakes for milder heat.

You need the fine, quick-cook variety of polenta for this; look at the packet and as long as the cooking time is 8 minutes or less, you're good to go. Coarse grind polenta that takes 40 minutes plus to cook won't work here.

200g fresh medium egg noodles or
   fresh spaghetti (if using dried
   egg noodles/spaghetti, see notes)
1 lemon: 1 teaspoon finely grated zest
   and 2 tablespoons juice
10g fresh chives, finely chopped
10g fresh dill, picked
full-fat crème fraîche or soured
   cream, to serve (optional)

Roasted mushrooms
400g oyster mushrooms
3 tablespoons olive oil
½ teaspoon fine salt

Sauce
40g unsalted butter
2 tablespoons olive oil, plus extra to serve
2 onions, very finely chopped
¾ teaspoon caraway seeds
1¼ teaspoon fine salt
2 cloves of garlic, finely grated/crushed
500g chicken stock (or veg stock/water)
2½ teaspoons English mustard
5 tablespoons double cream
freshly ground black pepper

Make ahead
The onions can be made up to a week
before and kept refrigerated. Bring back
to room temperature before using.

Notes
If you're starting with dried egg noodles/
spaghetti, cook until al dente before
adding to the sauce.

Oyster mushroom noodles with caramelised caraway onions

These noodles feature many ingredients typical of Eastern European cuisine: caraway seeds, fried onions, dill, sour cream. Inspired by mushroom pierogi, my hope was that this dish would taste a bit like a deconstructed version, although being extremely un-adept at Eastern European cooking, I wouldn't be at all surprised if I'm way off the mark. The fried onions steal the show, and require a little bit of patience to get them to be the golden jewels we're after. They need to be fried slowly over a medium heat to achieve a deep caramelisation – don't be tempted to turn up the heat to speed up the process.

Use plant-based alternatives to the dairy and noodles to keep this vegan.

———

Preheat the oven to 200°C fan/220°C.

First roast the mushrooms. Tear most of the mushrooms in half: if they're very small you can leave them whole, and if they're extra large, tear them into thirds. On a large, parchment-lined tray, mix the mushrooms with the oil and fine salt, then spread out. Roast for 22–25 minutes, stirring halfway, or until golden-brown and beginning to crisp around the edges. Set aside.

Meanwhile, make the sauce. Put the butter, oil, onions, caraway seeds and ¾ teaspoon of fine salt into a large sauté pan and place on a medium heat. You're after a slow, deep caramelisation here, so don't be tempted to turn the heat up to speed up that process. Gently fry for about 12 minutes, stirring often, until soft and golden. Turn the heat all the way down and continue to fry for 5 minutes; the onions should be deeply golden-brown and not at all burned or crispy. Transfer half the onions to a plate and set aside. Add the garlic to the remaining onions in the pan and fry for 1 minute, stirring often. Remove the pan from the heat.

Add the stock or water, mustard, cream, ½ teaspoon of fine salt and plenty of pepper to the pan with the remaining onions. Stir together, then add half the roasted mushrooms. Return to a medium heat and cook for 4 minutes. Stir the noodles or pasta into the sauce and cook for 3 minutes, or until the sauce has thickened slightly and the noodles are cooked through and hot.

Stir in the lemon juice and half the herbs. Top with the remaining herbs, the lemon zest and the mushrooms and onions you set aside earlier. Spoon over some crème fraîche or soured cream (if using), finish with olive oil and black pepper, and serve.

300g Thai sticky rice (aka glutinous
    rice or sweet rice) (see notes)
6 x 320g large beef tomatoes (1.9kg)
30g dried porcini, soaked in boiling water
20g fresh chives, finely chopped
2 tablespoons tomato purée/paste
1 teaspoon ground cumin
2 cloves of garlic, finely grated/crushed
6 tablespoons olive oil, plus extra to serve
120g ready-cooked peeled chestnuts,
    roughly chopped
fine salt
freshly ground black pepper

Tomatoes stuffed with
sticky porcini and chestnut rice

The use of sticky rice and dried mushrooms here is inspired by *lo mai gai* (a classic dim sum dish of sticky rice with chicken, sausage and dried shiitake mushrooms), although the unmistakable flavour of porcini and the sweetness of chestnuts take these stuffed tomatoes in a more Italian direction. Serve as an impressive vegan centrepiece or as a side.

———————

Put the rice into a container and cover with plenty of lukewarm water. Leave to soak for 1 hour, rinse well, drain and set aside. See notes – some sticky rice brands will need to be soaked overnight.

Preheat the oven to 190°C fan/210°C. While the rice is soaking, cut the tops off the tomatoes. Hollow them out over a container to collect the juice and pulp; use a small serrated knife and a spoon (or your hands) to do this, keeping the sides and bottoms about 1½cm thick, and trying your best not to puncture them. Don't throw away the tomato pulp and juice, you'll use both later.

Place the tomatoes in a medium, high-sided baking tray. Season the insides with ⅛ teaspoon of fine salt (each) and plenty of black pepper (about 30 twists in all).

Drain the porcini, then finely chop them and put them into a medium bowl. Add the drained rice, chives, tomato purée/paste, cumin, garlic, 3 tablespoons of oil, 1 teaspoon of fine salt and plenty of pepper. Very finely chop about 180g of the tomato pulp you scooped out earlier and add to the bowl of rice. Mix well, then fold in the chestnuts. Fill the tomatoes with the rice mixture – there should be enough to create a little dome in the top of each tomato. Pour 2 tablespoons of tomato juice into each tomato (use water if you don't have enough tomato juice), over the rice, then replace the tomato lid. Drizzle the tomatoes with 3 tablespoons of oil (in total) and season with ⅛ teaspoon of fine salt (each) and plenty of pepper.

Cover tightly with foil and bake for 25 minutes, then remove the foil and bake for another 35 minutes, basting the tomatoes in the last 10 minutes, until the rice inside is cooked through and the exposed rice is crispy. Don't worry if some of the tomatoes burst – this is a rustic dish!

Transfer the tomatoes to a platter. Add 2 tablespoons of tomato juice (or water, if you have none left) to the baking tray to help scrape up any sauce that has stuck to the tray. Pour the roasting juices around the tomatoes, finish with some extra olive oil, black pepper and flaked sea salt and serve.

Notes

I use the Thai Taste brand of sticky rice, which only needs to be soaked for 1 hour in order for it to cook through inside the tomatoes. If you're using another brand, check the side of the packet, as it may need to be soaked overnight.

5–6 large rainbow chard or Swiss chard
    leaves with stalks (about 220g/
    1 large bunch)
120g fresh lasagne sheets (about
    6 regular-sized sheets)

Rocket paste

60g rocket
15g fresh basil
3 anchovy fillets in olive oil
3 tablespoons olive oil
25g Parmesan, finely grated
1 teaspoon finely grated lemon zest
120g mascarpone
¼ teaspoon fine salt
plenty of freshly ground black pepper

Tomato sauce

400g tomato passata
40g unsalted butter, softened
1 large clove of garlic, finely grated/crushed
½ teaspoon fine salt
5g fresh oregano or basil sprigs
    (or both preferably)

Vegan option

Use plant-based alternatives to the dairy,
dry lasagne sheets and miso instead of
anchovies to make this vegan.

Make ahead

Prepare the rotolo up to 3 hours ahead
and keep covered until ready to bake.

Notes

I use shop-bought fresh lasagne sheets
here for ease. If you're starting with dry
lasagne sheets, you'll need to boil them
first until al dente, so they can be rolled.

Chard rotolo

Rotolo (meaning roll) is a lesser-known Italian dish consisting of a large sheet of pasta rolled with a spinach and ricotta filling. Traditionally the roll is wrapped in a tea towel and then boiled, but I've tried to simplify things here by baking it. Untraditionally, I've covered this rotolo with large chard leaves, which makes it look even more impressive than usual.

This recipe is not at all as complicated as it looks, and I've included step-by-step photos alongside the method here to prove it. You'll need large chard leaves, and they need to be blanched beforehand, because raw leaves won't cooperate when rolling, and the wetness of the blanched leaves helps everything stick together nicely. The rocket paste recipe is really just a blueprint; a good opportunity to use odds and ends of herbs and cheeses you might have in the fridge already, so feel free to mix it up. You can also add cooked ham to the layers if you like. The tomato sauce is intentionally simple, so as not to detract from the rotolo star of the show.

Preheat the oven to 200°C fan/220°C.

First make the rocket paste. You can do this by very finely chopping the rocket, basil and anchovies and mixing them with all the remaining ingredients to get a paste, or you can just stick the whole lot in a small food processor and pulse until smooth and combined.

Bring a large pot of water to the boil. Once boiling, blanch the chard leaves. Bunch the chard together and, holding the bunch by the stalks, dip the leaves into the boiling water up to the stalks for 30–40 seconds.

Transfer to a colander to drain away the excess water, then transfer to a chopping board and cut off the stalks, leaving the large leaves whole and intact. Very finely chop the stalks (they need to be really small), then stir them into the rocket paste.

Place the fresh lasagne sheets in a large heatproof container, cover with boiling water and leave to soften for a few minutes – this will make them easier to roll and stick. Drain well.

Continues on next page...

Chard rotolo continued...

Prepare your work surface with a large sheet of parchment paper. Lightly grease the parchment paper with oil. Very carefully to avoid ripping holes in them, lay the chard leaves on the parchment; arrange them so they are rib side up, overlapping, and with the stalk ends facing in alternating directions. (See photo, as this description makes it sound far more complicated than it actually is.)

Cover the leaves with a layer of overlapping lasagne sheets (see photo), then spread the rocket paste evenly over the sheets. With one of the shorter ends facing towards you, use the parchment paper to help you roll up the rotolo like a Swiss roll, keeping it as tight as possible. Make sure you end up with the seam side down. Tuck the leaves in at either end to stop the filling spilling out (see last photo).

Use the parchment paper to help you lift the rotolo into a large, high-sided baking tray. Cover tightly with foil and bake for 20 minutes, then remove the foil and bake for another 8 minutes. Set aside to rest for 15 minutes.

While the rotolo is resting, place all the ingredients for the sauce in a medium saucepan on a medium-high heat and cook for 15 minutes, turning the heat all the way down as soon as the sauce starts to spit. Discard the oregano/basil.

Pour the sauce on to a large platter. Cut the rotolo into thick slices and arrange on top of the sauce. Finish with olive oil and flaked salt, as always.

Gratin

900g cassava roots (for alternatives,
see notes)

3 large cloves of garlic,
finely grated/crushed

1 tablespoon white miso paste

1 medium onion, halved and very thinly
sliced on a mandolin (120g)

½ teaspoon medium curry powder

200g double cream

50g Parmesan, finely grated

40g ghee (from a jar not a tin, see page 17)
or unsalted butter, melted

1 teaspoon finely grated lemon zest

½ teaspoon fine sea salt

about 25 twists of freshly ground
black pepper

120g chicken stock (or veg stock/water)

Farofa (optional)

1 tablespoon olive oil

1 tablespoon ghee (from a jar not a tin,
see page 17) or unsalted butter

1 onion, very finely chopped

⅓ teaspoon fine salt

¼ teaspoon caraway seeds, roughly
crushed with a pestle and mortar

50g farofa, aka toasted coarse cassava
flour (or fine breadcrumbs)

Notes

Potato, golden sweet potato and cauliflower
will all work just as well as cassava (for the
cauliflower, you'll only need to blanch the
florets for 2 minutes). Use breadcrumbs
instead of farofa if you like, or just leave
out the crumb altogether.

Creamy cassava gratin with onion and caraway farofa

This gratin features my favourite root vegetable twice. The root is peeled, boiled and used in the gratin, then *farofa* – toasted coarse cassava flour – is used as a topping for the gratin. You can find cassava roots in most West African or Caribbean grocers and in some supermarkets, and *farofa* in any Brazilian shop or online. Having said that, I appreciate that both cassava and *farofa* are not only hard to find, but they will have also travelled from afar to get to the shelves (unless you're reading this in Brazil). You can absolutely use alternatives that are seasonal and grown locally to you (see notes).

———

Preheat the oven to 180°C fan/200°C. Use a very sharp peeler or a knife to peel the cassava roots, removing the thick brown skin as well as the layer of pink flesh beneath it. Don't use any part of the cassava that's blackened or soft. You should end up with about 700g. Cut the cassava into random bite-size chunks, about 4cm wide.

Bring a large pot of very well-salted water to the boil, then add the cassava and cook for 15 minutes, or until it is very soft and fluffy. Drain well. Some pieces of cassava will have a dry, stringy piece running through the centre – discard this.

In a medium bowl, mix together the rest of the ingredients for the gratin. Add the cooked cassava and gently mix together, trying not to break the chunks up.

Tip into a 20cm round baking dish (or a similar-sized dish), then place it on a flat tray to catch any liquid that bubbles over. Cover with foil and bake for 15 minutes, then remove from the oven, remove the foil and baste the surface with the creamy liquid. Return to the oven, uncovered and bake until golden-brown and bubbling, about 30 minutes, basting again halfway. Leave to rest for 10 minutes.

Meanwhile, make the farofa/breadcrumbs (if using). Place the oil, ghee, onion and fine salt into a medium, non-stick frying pan on a medium heat. Fry for 7 minutes, stirring often, until the onion is soft and lightly golden.

Reduce the heat to low, add the caraway seeds and continue to fry, stirring often, for 2–3 minutes, or until the onions are soft and deeply golden (take care not to burn them). Increase the heat to medium-high, add the farofa or breadcrumbs and stir-fry for 2 more minutes, until nicely toasted.

Top the gratin with some of the onion farofa, serving the rest on the side.

200g short-grain brown rice, soaked for
    at least 2 hours (preferably overnight)
8 red romano peppers
300g feta, roughly broken into
    small pieces
200g buffalo mozzarella, drained well,
    patted dry and torn into medium chunks
2 spring onions, julienned
5g fresh coriander leaves
2 limes, cut into wedges, to serve

Salsa roja
2 tablespoons olive oil
15g unsalted butter
1 medium onion, peeled and
    finely chopped (120g)
2 cloves of garlic, finely grated/crushed
300g sweet, ripe cherry tomatoes, such
    as Datterini
½ dried ancho chilli
1 dried habanero chilli (or a pinch
    of regular/chipotle chilli flakes,
    if you prefer milder heat)
1 teaspoon cumin seeds
½ teaspoon coriander seeds
1 teaspoon fine salt
120g water
2 teaspoons tomato purée/paste

Make ahead
Grill the peppers up to 2 days ahead. The
salsa roja will keep in the fridge for up to a
week. Prepare the peppers, up to the point
of stuffing them, up to 4 hours ahead.

Chiles rellenos with salsa roja risotto

Let's get a couple of things straight.

First, I know that these are not *chiles rellenos* in the true sense of the dish.
They are not made with Poblano chillies, they are not filled with traditional
ingredients,* they are not battered and deep-fried. They are, however, inspired
by *chiles rellenos* (one of my favourite dishes of all time) and they are also, quite
literally, *chiles rellenos* – stuffed (chilli) peppers.**

Second, I also know that this is not risotto – it is not made with arborio rice, and
it is not cooked in the traditional manner. However, the texture of the end result
is very much like that of a good risotto. It would be remiss of me to call this dish
something like … oh, I don't know, *'Stuffed peppers with spicy rice'*. Not only
does that sound really boring, it also takes away from that crucial inspiration.

*Although if you can get your hands on *queso Oaxaca/quesillo*, please use this
instead of feta and mozzarella.

** I used romano peppers because they are a readily available, flavoursome
pepper variety in the UK. If you have access to fresh Poblano chilli peppers,
please use them instead.

––––––––––

First make sure to soak the rice for at least 2 hours, or overnight. When you're
ready to start cooking, turn the oven grill to the highest setting.

Cut a slit along one side of each pepper, keeping them attached at the top and
bottom. Arrange the peppers on a rack set over a baking tray, slit-side up.

Grill until soft and blackened in patches, about 7 minutes, then turn the peppers
and grill for another 4–8 minutes, until that side is soft and blackened in patches
too. Keep an eye on them, as they may be ready sooner if your grill runs hot. Set
the tray aside and leave the peppers to cool on the rack, slit side down, so any
liquid drains away.

Cook the rice. Drain the soaked rice and put into a medium saucepan with
450g of water. Bring to a simmer over a medium-high heat. Once simmering,
lower the heat to low, cover the pan with a lid, and cook for 25 minutes.
Remove from the heat and leave to rest for 10 minutes with the lid still on.

Continues on next page...

Chiles rellenos continued...

While the rice is cooking, make the salsa. Put the first 10 ingredients (everything except the water and tomato purée/paste) into a large sauté pan on a medium-high heat and fry, stirring often, for 15 minutes, until the tomatoes have broken down and the onions are soft and golden-brown. Turn the heat down to medium or medium-low if the mixture starts to catch or burn.

Discard the habanero (or squeeze it with the back of a spoon before removing it if you like heat). Transfer the salsa to a blender with the water and tomato purée/paste and blend until completely smooth. Return to the pan and set aside.

Turn the oven grill to the highest setting.

Now stuff the peppers. Mix the feta and mozzarella together in a bowl. Transfer the peppers from the rack to a foil-lined tray. Peel some of the skin off – just the bits that tear away easily (you don't want to rip a hole in the peppers). Pat the insides dry and season with a pinch of salt. Stuff the peppers with the cheese mixture. Sprinkle with a little flaked salt and drizzle over a little oil. You can prepare the peppers up to this point up to 4 hours ahead.

Grill for 7–9 minutes near the top of the oven, until the cheese is bubbling and browned in patches. Set aside to cool for a few minutes (but not for too long, as the melted cheese will begin to harden).

Add the cooked rice to the pan with the salsa roja, stir together and gently heat through for a minute. The texture should be that of a loose, saucy risotto; add a splash of water if it's looking thick.

To serve, spoon the risotto onto a platter and top with the peppers. Finish with the spring onions and coriander, squeeze over some lime and serve.

Roasted mushrooms

500g brown chestnut
    mushrooms, quartered

300g oyster mushrooms, torn in
    half or into quarters if large

50g soy sauce or tamari

2 teaspoons white miso paste

90g olive oil

4 large cloves of garlic, finely
    grated/crushed

40g tomato purée/paste

50g maple syrup

5g fresh sage leaves

5g fresh basil leaves

2 tablespoons water

¾ teaspoon ground cumin

⅓ teaspoon fine salt

about 30 twists of freshly
    ground black pepper

Dough

200g '00' flour

4g fast-action dried yeast
    (about 1 teaspoon)

¾ teaspoon caster sugar

½ teaspoon fine salt

140g lukewarm water

½ teaspoon ground cumin

about 30 twists of freshly
    ground black pepper

Wash

1 tablespoon plant-based milk

½ tablespoon olive oil

15g toasted sesame seeds

Salsa verde

10g fresh chives, finely chopped

5g fresh parsley, finely chopped

3 tablespoons olive oil

½ tablespoon lemon juice

½ small clove of garlic, very finely chopped

⅛ teaspoon fine salt

Giant mushroom and sesame roll with salsa verde

This impressive vegan centrepiece is inspired by Celebration sticky rice cake, one of the last recipes I developed at the OTK (Ottolenghi Test Kitchen). Both recipes feature mushrooms that are roasted to create not only the bulk of the dish, but also the gravy. The dough here features a few times throughout **MEZCLA** in slightly different guises, highlighting its versatility. You can see it on page 179 in the form of Fried bread and on page 276 in the form of a Coconut, chocolate and coffee roll. Admittedly this is a long recipe, but I assure you the result is well worth the effort.

Preheat the oven to 220°C fan/240°C. Put all the ingredients for the roasted mushrooms into a 30 x 20cm non-stick, high-sided baking tray and mix well. The size and height of the tray is important here – if it's any bigger and not high-sided, you won't create the environment you need to make the mushroom gravy. Roast for 15 minutes, then remove from the oven.

Transfer the mushrooms to a sieve set over a medium saucepan, so all the liquid – which will be your gravy – drains into the saucepan. Help things along by giving the mushrooms a really good squeeze. You should end up with about 110g of liquid in the pan, but if you have any less, supplement with equal amounts of soy sauce and water. Set the saucepan aside until later.

Return the squeezed mushrooms to the tray, spread out, and roast for another 5 minutes. Set aside to cool completely. Switch the oven off, leaving the door open so it cools down.

Put all the ingredients for the dough into the bowl of a stand mixer and knead on medium-high speed for 10 minutes. If you don't have a mixer, bring the ingredients together in a bowl, then transfer to a work surface lightly greased with olive oil and knead for 15 minutes. The resulting dough should be smooth and pliable.

Tip the dough on to a lightly oiled surface. Lightly grease your mixing bowl with olive oil. Shape the dough into a smooth, round mass and return it to the bowl. Lightly grease the surface of the dough with some olive oil to stop it drying out, then cover with a damp cloth. Place the bowl in the cool, switched-off oven (make sure it's only *just* warm and not still hot, otherwise wait a bit longer before placing the bowl in the oven). Close the door and leave to prove for 1 hour, or until doubled in size.

Continues on next page...

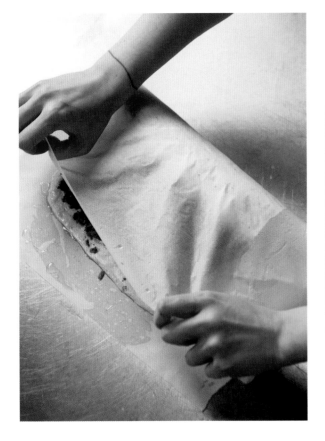

Giant mushroom roll continued...

Very finely chop the roasted mushrooms to a mince consistency – you can easily do this by pulsing a few times in a food processor, if you have one. Set aside.

Place a large piece of non-stick parchment paper on your work surface and lightly grease it with olive oil. Tip the proved dough on to your oily paper. Use your hands to press the dough out into a 35 x 23cm rectangle; the dough will spring back at first, but keep on stretching it into a rectangle until it stops springing back. Make sure the thickness of the dough is as even as possible, and patch up any holes that form by pinching the dough back together. Scatter the mushrooms evenly over to cover the dough.

Starting at one of the shorter ends, use the oily paper to help you roll the dough up like a Swiss roll, making sure you end up with the seam of the dough underneath. Tuck the dough in and under at either end of the roll, so the filling doesn't spill out. Use the parchment to help you lift the roll on to a flat baking tray, again ensuring that the roll is seam side down. If there are any holes in the dough, pinch them together.

Return the roll uncovered to the cool, switched-off oven, close the door and prove for another 30 minutes, or until significantly puffed up.

Remove the tray from the oven and set aside. Preheat the oven to 180°C fan/200°C.

For the wash, mix the milk and oil together. Brush the roll all over with the milk mixture, then sprinkle the sesame seeds to cover the roll, pressing them into the surface so they stick.

Make ahead

Roast the mushrooms, pour off the gravy and then chop the mushrooms up to 2 days before. Store the chopped mushrooms and the mushroom gravy in the fridge separately, bringing them back to room temperature while the dough proves. If you've got ahead by roasting the mushrooms, you'll need to preheat the oven to the lowest temperature (no higher than 50°C) before switching off the oven and proving the dough inside it.

Make the dough a day ahead and, after the first prove, keep refrigerated in a large, sealed container. Bring back to room temperature before stretching out into a rectangle and filling it.

Once the oven is hot, bake the roll for 30 minutes, rotating the tray halfway so it colours evenly. Lower the heat to 170°C fan/190°C and bake for another 10 minutes until golden brown. The surface of the roll will feel quite hard to the touch at this point, but it will soften as it cools. Remove from the oven and leave to cool for 10 minutes. If you have one, use a blowtorch to lightly char the sesame seeds. Sprinkle with flaked salt.

Mix all the ingredients for the salsa together.

Place the pan with the mushroom gravy on a medium heat and cook until heated through. Give it a good mix to combine the oil and the mushroom juices.

Cut the roll into thick slices and serve with the salsa verde and mushroom gravy.

Roasted veg

1kg kohlrabi (about 2–3), peeled and
	cut into 2cm chunks (700g)

400g sweet, ripe cherry tomatoes,
	such as Datterini

1 large mild red chilli, quartered (optional)

3 tablespoons olive oil

1¼ teaspoons fine salt

freshly ground black pepper

Ginger and tomato broth

50g fresh ginger, peeled and julienned

1 teaspoon fine salt

4 tablespoons olive oil

1 tablespoon white miso paste

3 tablespoons tomato purée/paste

1 clove of garlic, finely grated/crushed

900g water (or chicken stock)

1 tablespoon lemon juice

To serve

crème fraîche (regular or plant-based)

5g fresh chives, roughly chopped

5g fresh mint leaves

5g fresh coriander leaves

5g fresh basil leaves

Roasted kohlrabi and tomato broth with crispy ginger

Ginger is used twice here: first to flavour the oil in which you cook the broth, then to add crunch before serving.

The broth is wonderful in its own right, and if you don't have the time to roast vegetables, you can instead just poach things quickly in the flavoursome liquid; anything from fish, prawns, clams and tofu to sliced leafy greens will work well. To bulk up this stew, add fresh udon noodles or jarred beans. I like to serve a big plate of freshly washed and still-wet herbs on the side, reminiscent of the plate of herbs you'd get with a Vietnamese *pho*, for you to add as you please.

———————

Preheat the oven to 200°C fan/220°C.

First make the roasted veg. Line a large, flat baking tray with parchment paper. Put the kohlrabi, tomatoes, chilli, oil, salt and pepper on the tray and mix well. Roast for about 40–50 minutes, gently stirring a couple of times, until the kohlrabi is well browned and the tomatoes are soft and a little charred. Set aside.

Meanwhile, make the broth. Toss the ginger with ¼ teaspoon of fine salt. Put the olive oil into a medium saucepan on a medium-low heat with one piece of the ginger. Once the ginger starts to sizzle, add the rest of the ginger to the oil and gently fry, stirring constantly with a fork to separate the pieces, until the ginger is crisp and light golden. This should take about 3½ minutes, but keep a close eye on it as it can turn from golden to brown and burnt quite quickly. Remove the pan from the heat, then remove the crispy ginger with a fork or slotted spoon, transfer to a small plate and set aside.

Off the heat (as the oil will still be very hot), add the miso, tomato purée/paste and garlic to the pan of ginger oil and cook in the residual heat, stirring often, for 1 minute. Return to a medium heat and continue to fry, stirring every now and then, for 2 minutes.

Increase the heat to medium-high and add the stock or water, lemon juice and ¾ teaspoon of fine salt. Bring to a simmer and cook for 12 minutes.

Once roasted, divide the vegetables between four bowls, then spoon over the hot broth. Top with a spoonful of the crème fraîche, followed by the crispy ginger. Serve the herbs on the side, to add to the soup as you go.

Make ahead

The broth will keep in the fridge for up to a week (although the fried ginger will only remain crispy for a day).

750g sweet potatoes, peeled and cut
 into 4mm-thick slices on a mandolin
 or by hand
2 limes, cut into wedges, to serve

Red curry sauce
2 x 400g tins of full-fat coconut milk
 (at least 70% coconut extract)
150g sweet, ripe cherry tomatoes,
 such as Datterini
2–3 large mild red chillies (deseed or
 add less if you prefer less heat),
 roughly chopped (30g)
25g fresh ginger, peeled and
 roughly chopped
4 cloves of garlic, roughly chopped
1 banana shallot, roughly chopped
1 stick of lemongrass, outer layer removed,
 roughly chopped
5g fresh lime leaves, stalks discarded
2 teaspoons tomato purée/paste
1½ tablespoons maple syrup
1 tablespoon soy sauce
1¼ teaspoons fine salt

Fried aromatics (optional)
4 tablespoons olive oil
20g fresh ginger, peeled and julienned
5g fresh Thai basil leaves

Notes
The fried aromatics are optional,
although they do make the gratin look
really beautiful, while adding a lovely
crunch. If you'd rather not make them,
just use regular olive oil every time
I call for 'aromatic oil'.

Red curry sweet potato gratin

This tastes a bit like a Panang curry, but in gratin form. Serve it as an impressive vegan main course with a salad or some sautéd greens, as a side dish with meat or fish, or as part of a spread.

———————

Preheat the oven to 200°C fan/220°C.

Pour both tins of coconut milk into a bowl and whisk until smooth. Transfer half (400g) of the coconut milk to a serving bowl and set aside. Pour the remaining 400g of coconut milk into a blender with all of the ingredients for the red curry sauce and blitz until completely smooth.

Lightly grease a round 28cm ovenproof high-sided pan or dish. Put the sweet potatoes and curry sauce into a large bowl and use your hands to mix the two together so the slices are completely covered with sauce. Tip it all into the pan/ dish and level everything out. Make sure the surface is completely covered with sauce by pushing down on the slices to submerge the top layer.

Cover tightly with a lid/foil and bake for 40 minutes.

While the gratin is in the oven, fry the aromatics (if making). Prepare a heatproof sieve set over a heatproof bowl. Put the oil into a small saucepan on a medium-high heat along with one piece of the ginger. Once the ginger starts to sizzle, drop in the rest of the ginger and fry for about 1 minute 45 seconds, swirling the pan every now and then to separate the pieces. Add the basil and fry for another 30 seconds, swirling the pan, then remove from the heat and strain through the sieve set over the bowl. Transfer the aromatics to a plate and spread out. Reserve the aromatic oil.

After 40 minutes, remove the foil from the gratin and use the back of a large spoon to push down on the surface and submerge the top layer in sauce again. Drizzle with 1½ tablespoons of the aromatic oil. Return to the oven for 25 minutes uncovered, then turn the oven to the highest grill setting and grill for about 6 minutes, or until beginning to crisp and turn golden-brown on top. Keep an eye on the gratin, as some grills are much hotter than others.

Spoon over 4 tablespoons of the reserved coconut milk, followed by 1½ tablespoons of the aromatic oil. Finish with the crispy aromatics and serve with the lime wedges and the remaining coconut milk alongside, for drizzling over as you eat.

Makes 6 pieces

1 litre sunflower oil, for frying

flaked salt

Dough

200g '00' flour

4g fast-action dried yeast

¾ teaspoon caster sugar

½ teaspoon fine salt

140g lukewarm water

olive oil, for greasing

Make ahead

Make the dough the day before, leave it to prove as in the recipe, then transfer to the fridge and leave overnight. The next day, remove from the fridge and proceed with the recipe.

Notes

Prove your dough near a warm radiator or in your boiler cupboard. If neither of those are convenient, preheat your oven at the lowest setting for 10 minutes, then switch it off and place your covered bowl of dough inside to rise.

This image also shows Pineapple pizza salsa, see page 71.

Fried bread to go with just about anything

In Naples and the south of Italy, pizza dough is sometimes fried instead of baked, resulting in a deliciously donut-like savoury, bubbly, crispy dough. Serve alongside the Cheesy roasted aubergines on page 24, with any of the dips in the book, or with the Pineapple pizza salsa (pictured opposite, recipe on page 71). I like to blowtorch the bread after it's been fried, so it tastes both deep-fried and charred. I've said it before and I'll say it again, I highly recommend you get a blowtorch, it's truly one of the best kitchen tools.

———————

Preheat the oven to the very lowest temperature (no higher than 50°C). Put all the ingredients for the dough into the bowl of a stand mixer with the dough hook attached and knead on medium-high speed for 10 minutes. If you don't have a mixer, bring the ingredients together in a bowl, then transfer to a work surface lightly dusted with flour and knead for 15 minutes. The resulting dough should be smooth, pliable and slightly sticky. Turn the oven off.

Tip the dough out onto your work surface and shape it into a smooth, round shape. Lightly grease your mixing bowl, then return the dough to it. Lightly grease the surface of the dough with olive oil to stop it drying out, then cover with a damp cloth. Place the bowl in the switched-off, cool oven and leave to prove for 1 hour, or until doubled in size.

Grease your work surface with olive oil, then lift the dough out on to it. With a sharp knife or dough cutter, divide the dough into 6 equal pieces weighing about 55g each.

Roll each piece into a smooth ball, then transfer to a lightly greased tray. Lightly grease each ball with a little olive oil, then return to the switched-off oven, uncovered, and leave to prove for another 30 minutes to 1 hour, or until doubled in size.

Fill a large saucepan or wok with the frying oil and place on a medium-high heat. Prepare a tray lined with kitchen paper or a clean absorbent cloth. Lightly grease your work surface with olive oil.

Test the oil is hot enough by dropping in a small piece of dough. If it sizzles and rises to the top straight away, you're ready to start shaping and frying. If you have a temperature probe, the oil should be at 180°C.

Continues on next page...

Fried bread continued...

Take a piece of dough and stretch it into a 12cm rough circle. It will spring back the first time you stretch it, but once you stretch it out a few more times it should keep its shape. Poke the centre of the dough about 5 times with a sharp knife. Shape another piece before frying.

Fry two pieces of dough at a time. Lower the dough into the oil and fry for about 1½–2 minutes on each side, using a slotted spoon or spider to hold the dough under the surface of the oil as it fries, until puffed up and golden-brown all over. Transfer to the paper-lined tray and sprinkle with flaked salt. Continue with the rest of the dough in the same way.

If you have a blowtorch, char the fried bread in places once they've been fried, so they taste both deep-fried and charred.

FISH

Prawn dumplings and creamed corn

Dumplings

300g raw peeled king prawns (about
 600g if starting with shell-on prawns)

1 clove of garlic, finely grated/crushed

5g fresh chives, finely chopped

¼ teaspoon smoked paprika

1 teaspoon finely grated lemon zest

½ teaspoon fine salt

1 tablespoon olive oil, plus extra
 for rolling

2 limes, cut into wedges, to serve

Spicy tomato butter sauce

3 tablespoons olive oil

30g unsalted butter

4 cloves of garlic, very finely chopped

1 mild red chilli, finely chopped

½ Scotch bonnet chilli, finely chopped
 (optional, only if you like heat)

½ teaspoon fine salt

100g sweet, ripe cherry tomatoes,
 such as Datterini, finely chopped

½ teaspoon tomato purée/paste

½ teaspoon smoked paprika

5g fresh chives, finely chopped

freshly ground black pepper

Creamed corn

350g frozen corn, defrosted

30g unsalted butter

80g Greek-style yoghurt

80g Gruyère, finely grated

¾ teaspoon ground cumin

¾ teaspoon fine salt

300g chicken stock or water (or shellfish
 stock made from the prawn shells)

40g instant, quick-cook polenta (check
 the pack, you need a polenta that
 cooks in 8 minutes or less, not the
 coarse variety that takes 40 minutes)

This recipe is inspired by shrimp and grits, a dish typical of the Carolinas, Georgia and Louisiana, consisting of milled corn, shrimp and a Southern blend of herbs and spices. It's a dish I've never actually tried, but have always lusted over.

In this version the prawns are turned into dumplings, and I use a combination of fresh corn, polenta and Gruyère for the 'grits' element. I've suggested using ready-peeled raw prawns for ease, but by all means start with shell-on prawns if you prefer. You can then make a stock out of the shells and heads, and use that in the creamed corn in place of water.

If you're short on time, skip the part where you turn the prawns into dumplings. Mix the whole, peeled prawns with the remaining dumpling ingredients, then fry them for a few minutes until *just* cooked. Transfer the cooked prawns to a plate and proceed with making the sauce.

———————

Finely chop the prawns into a rough mash, then put them into a bowl with the remaining dumpling ingredients, except for the olive oil. Combine thoroughly.

Divide the prawn mixture into 8 portions each weighing 35–40g. Grease your hands with oil and roll each portion into a smooth, compacted ball.

Put 1 tablespoon of olive oil into a medium (28cm) non-stick frying pan on a medium-high heat. Once the oil is very hot, fry the dumplings for 5 minutes, turning regularly with tongs, until nicely browned all over. Remove the pan from the heat, transfer the dumplings to a bowl and cover with a plate. Don't wash the pan, you'll use it to make the sauce.

For the sauce, add the olive oil and the butter to the pan and return it to a medium-low heat. Once the butter has melted, add the garlic, both chillies and the fine salt and very gently fry for 3–4 minutes, stirring often, until the garlic is soft and fragrant. You don't want the garlic to brown or fry, so turn the heat down if necessary.

Remove the pan from the heat and stir in the tomatoes, tomato purée/paste, paprika, the chives and plenty of black pepper. Place the dumplings in the sauce, cover with a lid or foil and set aside while you make the corn.

Continues on next page...

Prawn dumplings continued...

For the creamed corn, blitz the corn in a processor (or very finely chop as much as you can by hand) to get a wet mash. Transfer the corn to a large sauté pan with the butter, yoghurt, Gruyère, cumin, salt, stock or water and polenta.

Mix well, then place on a medium-high heat. Cook for 7–8 minutes, stirring constantly, until the mixture thickens to porridge consistency – as soon as the mixture starts to spit, turn the heat all the way down.

Place the pan with the dumplings and sauce on a medium heat with the lid on and warm through for a few minutes.

Serve at once. Spoon the polenta on to a large, lipped platter or individual shallow bowls. Top with the sauce and dumplings and squeeze over the lime wedges.

Make ahead

Mix and shape the dumplings the day before. Keep refrigerated and bring them back to room temperature before frying.

Moqueca fish pie

Moqueca

400g skinless, boneless fish fillets
    cut into 4cm chunks (I like to use
    a mix of trout and hake)

150g raw peeled king prawns

1 tablespoon olive oil

50g unrefined sustainable red palm oil
    (see intro for alternatives)

4 cloves of garlic, very finely chopped
    (not crushed!)

1 yellow (or red) romano pepper,
    chopped into 1cm pieces (120g)

1 red chilli, finely chopped
    (deseeded if you like)

1 Scotch bonnet chilli, whole
    and unpierced (optional)

150g sweet, ripe cherry tomatoes,
    such as Datterini, halved

2 teaspoons tomato purée/paste

1¼ teaspoons smoked paprika

400g tin of full-fat coconut milk
    (at least 70% coconut extract)

40g fine, quick-cook polenta (or coarse
    cassava flour if you can find it)

5g fresh coriander, roughly chopped

10g spring onions, finely chopped

1 tablespoon lime juice

fine salt

Potato topping

700g red-skinned potatoes (or another
    good mashing potato), peeled and
    roughly chopped (600g)

50g olive oil

60g milk

shop-bought fried potato sticks
    (aka *batata palha*), to serve (optional)

Moqueca is a traditional Brazilian seafood stew flavoured with red palm oil (see page 15), coconut milk and lime. It's one of my favourite dishes, often served alongside *pirão* (a savoury porridge of sorts made by beating coarse cassava flour into hot seafood stock). Both these dishes are said to have originated with indigenous Brazilians; however, they have been enhanced by enslaved people from Africa, who shaped Brazil's culinary identity, permeating the essence of Brazilian cooking with African soul. *Azeite de dendê* (red palm oil) is an example of an ingredient that is native to West Africa but is now ubiquitous in Brazilian cooking. The flavour of red palm oil is hard to describe; it's savoury without being salty, almost like ghee flavoured with carrot and mild paprika, but also nothing like that at all. If you can find an unrefined, sustainable brand, it's well worth experimenting with. Ghee or butter, with an extra pinch of paprika for colour, can be used in its place. Here I turn this traditional Brazilian stew into an English-style fish pie with the addition of a mashed potato topping – it's Brazilian-English fusion, just like me.

Put the fish and prawns into a container with ¾ teaspoon of fine salt. Gently stir and set aside to lightly cure while you make the rest, or for up to 3 hours.

Place the potatoes in a medium saucepan, cover with room temperature water and plenty of salt. Bring to a simmer and cook until the potatoes are very soft all the way through. Drain well, then return to the pan with the oil and milk and mash until as smooth as possible. For best results, use a potato ricer if you have one. Add more salt to taste, if needed.

Preheat the oven to its highest grill setting.

Put the oil and the palm oil (or ghee/butter) into a large sauté pan and place on a medium heat. Once melted, add the garlic, romano pepper, both chillies and 1 teaspoon of fine salt to the pan. Gently fry for 5 minutes, stirring often, until the peppers are beginning to soften and the garlic is fragrant. You don't want the garlic to brown, so turn the heat down if necessary.

Add the tomatoes, tomato purée/paste and smoked paprika. Stir-fry for 2 minutes, then stir in the coconut milk and simmer for 4 minutes. Discard the Scotch bonnet (squeeze it into the sauce first if you like heat). Add the polenta and cook for 2 minutes, stirring constantly, until the sauce begins to thicken.

Continues on next page...

Moqueca fish pie continued...

Stir in the coriander, spring onion, lime juice and the marinated fish and prawns and transfer the mixture to a 20cm round baking dish or ovenproof pan, spreading the seafood out evenly.

Spoon the potato mixture on top, leaving gaps here and there for the sauce to bubble through. Don't flatten the surface, you want hills of potato that will crisp up under the grill. Drizzle with oil, then grill near the top of the oven until golden-brown and crisp on top, about 10 minutes, but this may take more or less time depending on your grill. The heat of the sauce combined with the heat of the grill should cook the fish through. If you don't have a working grill, bake at 230°C fan/250°C for 10–12 minutes, or until golden-brown and bubbling.

Leave to cool for 10 minutes, then cover with some fried potato sticks, if using, and serve with lime wedges.

Notes

For a quicker meal, serve this as a seafood stew with rice or salad, rather than as a pie. You won't need the potatoes, in that case, and you also won't need to add the polenta/cassava (which acts as a thickener for the pie base but is not needed otherwise). Poach the marinated fish and seafood in the broth for a few minutes before serving.

Hake torta ahogada with prawn miso bisque

Torta ahogada, meaning drowned sandwich, is a classic Mexican snack from the state of Jalisco, best eaten – in my opinion and from personal experience – at night when you're very, very drunk. You *absolutely* need to eat this with your hands, letting the sauce ooze down your chin and inevitably, down your wrists and into your shirt. If you're doing it right, the sauce might even find its way to your armpits. The hake torta and prawn bisque are a match made in heaven, but you can also just make one or the other, if you prefer. The torta is great with just a squeeze of lime, and the bisque can be tossed through pasta or used as a base for a seafood stew. If you're not serving the bisque with the hake (which is in itself very limey) you'll need to finish the bisque with a good squeeze of lemon or lime juice.

Prawn miso bisque

- 400g large, shell-on and head-on prawns
- 120g olive oil
- 5 cloves of garlic, roughly chopped
- 1½ teaspoons fine salt
- 1 tablespoon white miso paste
- 140g tomato purée/paste (260g total if you can't get hold of red pepper paste, see below)
- 120g mild Turkish red pepper paste (or use an extra 120g tomato purée/paste if you can't find any)
- 1–2 dried habanero chillies, whole and unpierced
- 1.5 litres water
- 200g sweet, ripe cherry tomatoes, such as Datterini, halved
- fish heads/bones from your fishmonger (optional)
- freshly ground black pepper

Hake in lime butter

- 400g hake (or cod/pollock/halibut), cut into 2cm pieces
- 1 teaspoon caster sugar
- 1 tablespoon olive oil
- 110g unsalted butter
- ½ large onion, peeled and very finely chopped (80g)
- 4 small cloves of garlic, finely chopped (not crushed!)
- 1 Scotch bonnet chilli, whole and unpierced (optional)
- 60g lime juice
- fine salt

To serve

- 6 small brioche rolls
- 2 teaspoons fresh chives, finely chopped
- lime wedges

Put the whole prawns (shells and heads left on) into a food processor with the oil, garlic, salt, miso, tomato purée/paste and red pepper paste. Pulse until combined into a rough paste. If you don't have a food processor, roughly chop the prawns (you'll need a sharp knife to get through the shells and heads), then mix with the remaining ingredients.

Heat a large, non-stick, high-sided sauté or saucepan on a high heat, then add the prawn mixture to the pan along with the habaneros (use 1 for medium heat and 2 for hot). Fry, stirring often, for 8 minutes, until the prawn shells and heads turn pink and everything is bubbling and fragrant. Turn down the heat if the mixture starts to catch or burn.

After about 8 minutes, turn the heat up to high and pour over the water. Whisk to combine, then add the tomatoes and any other fish heads/bones you might have, season with plenty of black pepper and bring to a simmer. Once simmering, reduce the heat to medium and simmer for 25 minutes, skimming off any scum that collects at the top.

Take the pan off the heat and leave to cool for 10 minutes. Strain the liquid through a large sieve set over a large saucepan – this can get messy, so it's best done in the sink. Use a potato masher or whisk to mash the solids through the sieve, making sure all the liquid and flavour is released into the pan below – this can take a few minutes. Once you're sure you've extracted as much liquid as possible, the solids can be discarded. Strain the liquid once again to get rid of any remaining solids, then return to the saucepan.

Continues on next page...

Hake torta ahogada continued...

Place the pan on a medium-high heat and simmer until reduced to a thin soup consistency. This should take about 12 minutes and you should have about 750g when you're done. Set aside to cool while you prepare the hake. You'll only need about 300g of the bisque for the tortas, the rest can be frozen or refrigerated for another recipe.

Put the hake pieces into a container with the sugar, oil and 1 teaspoon of fine salt. Gently mix together, being careful not to break any of the pieces, then leave to cure while you prepare the rest.

Preheat the oven to 170°C fan/190°C.

Put the butter, onion, garlic, Scotch bonnet (if using), lime juice and ½ teaspoon of fine salt into a medium saucepan on a medium-low heat and very gently cook for 8–10 minutes, until the onion is very, very soft. You don't want the mixture to fry or brown, so turn the heat down if necessary.

Stir in the hake and cook, stirring gently, for about 1 minute and 30 seconds, until just cooked. Transfer the hake along with all the sauce to a bowl to stop it cooking any further.

Remove the Scotch bonnet. If you like extra heat, halve it so you can discard the seeds and pith, then very finely chop the flesh and mix about half the chopped chilli into the hake mixture.

Slice the brioche rolls open along the top, then place on a tray in the preheated oven for 5 minutes, or until warmed through.

Warm up the bisque.

Stuff the rolls with the hake, along with the oniony, limey butter. Sprinkle with chives and serve alongside bowls of the bisque for dipping, and lime wedges for squeezing over.

950g side of good-quality, sustainable
    salmon, rainbow trout or sea trout

250g mild olive oil

5g fresh coriander, leaves and stalks

5g fresh Thai (or regular) basil leaves
    and stalks

lime wedges, to serve

Tomato, lemongrass and lime leaf salsa

150g sweet, ripe cherry tomatoes,
    such as Datterini

2–3 large mild red chillies, deseeded
    and roughly chopped (30g)

25g fresh ginger, peeled and
    roughly chopped

4 cloves of garlic, roughly chopped

1 small banana shallot, peeled and
    roughly chopped (40g)

15g fresh lemongrass, outer layer
    discarded, finely chopped

5g fresh lime leaves, stalks removed,
    roughly chopped

1 tablespoon tomato purée/paste (20g)

2 tablespoons maple syrup

2 tablespoons soy sauce

3 tablespoons lime juice

½ teaspoon green (or black)
    peppercorns, roughly crushed

2½ teaspoons fine salt

Herb salad

½ cucumber, peeled, halved and
    watery centre scraped out

½ red onion, thinly sliced (60g)

20g fresh coriander leaves

10g fresh mint leaves

5g fresh Thai basil leaves

2 tablespoons lime juice

⅛ teaspoon fine salt

Celebration salmon

Fit for a celebration, this dish is a joy to look at, a joy to eat, and what's more it's incredibly easy to make, which is a celebration in itself. You could use either salmon or trout here, but it's important to use a very good-quality side of fish, and to make sure that it's sustainable, which is another reason I suggest that this is a celebration dish, rather than one you cook all the time. Having said that, you can absolutely use the same salsa and cooking application on other sustainable fillets of fish, more often (see notes).

The fish is confit (slow cooked in oil), so it's only just cooked and still very pink and moist inside. This is intentional, but you can cook it for up to 15 minutes longer, if you prefer. For the olive oil, make sure you use something mild, rather than a peppery extra virgin olive oil.

Serve with the Sticky coconut rice cake (without the tomatoes) (page 124) or with fresh corn tortillas (page 143). For tacos, flake the fish into large chunks and pile on to warm tortillas. Top with the tomato lemongrass salsa, a squeeze of lime and the salad.

Reuse the oil for up to 3 days – strain it first to remove any solids, and keep it in the fridge. Use it in stir-fries, fried rice, pasta, noodles, or to make aïoli or rouille.

———

You'll need a 34 x 26cm high-sided baking tray. Ideally your tray shouldn't be any bigger, otherwise you'll need more oil, and the flavour of the sauce will be diluted. Pat the salmon dry and place in the tray, skin side down (it will fit best diagonally). Pour over the 250g of olive oil – it won't cover the salmon completely but that's fine.

Put all the ingredients for the salsa into a food processor and pulse until the solids are very finely chopped (very finely chop the ingredients by hand if you don't have a processor). Pour the salsa over the salmon and into the oil, making sure the flesh side is completely covered in salsa. Add the 5g of coriander and 5g of basil to the oil.

Cover tightly with foil and place on the middle shelf of a cold oven. Immediately turn the oven to 80°C fan/100°C. Cook for 45 minutes, or until the thickest part of the salmon is *just* cooked, but still quite pink. (If you don't like your fish pink, cook it for a further 10–15 minutes.) Remove from the oven and set aside, still covered, for another 15 minutes.

While the salmon is resting, make the salad. Slice the cucumber on the diagonal and toss with the remaining salad ingredients.

Carefully transfer the salmon to a platter using 2 wide spatulas. You might want to ask for some help doing this as the salmon is very delicate. Strain the oil and salsa in the tray through a sieve set over a bowl. Discard the cooked herbs. Make sure the salmon is covered in salsa, and transfer any remaining salsa to a serving bowl. Spoon some of the aromatic oil over and around the salmon. Store any remaining oil in a clean glass jar – see bottom of intro.

Serve the salmon with the salad, lime wedges and remaining salsa on the side.

Notes

Use other fish varieties, if you like. For smaller sides of fish weighing around 700g, confit for 30 minutes. For fillets weighing around 100g each, confit for 20 minutes. If your side of fish is over 1kg, confit for another 10 minutes per 200g.

Use any leftover fish, salsa and oil to make fried rice. Fry some garlic and finely chopped spring onions in leftover confit oil (strained, see recipe introduction), then add some of the leftover salsa, followed by some flaked fish. Stir-fry for a few minutes before adding cooked rice and frying until it begins to crisp up. Stir through herbs (like coriander, chives or spring onions) and squeeze over plenty of lime before serving.

Scallops with curried onions and lime

12 medium–large scallops, at room
  temperature (remove the orange
  roe if serving raw)
2 tablespoons olive oil
½ teaspoon fine salt
1 dried habanero chilli (optional)
1 lime, cut into wedges, to serve
freshly ground black pepper

Curried onions

50g unsalted butter, in chunks
3 onions, finely chopped (440g)
1⅛ teaspoons fine salt
5 tablespoons olive oil
1 teaspoon medium curry powder

I love the combination of browned butter, curry, onion and lime here. It pairs perfectly with the scallops, which can be fried as per the method below, or served raw (in which case remove the orange roe). There's nothing particularly complicated about this recipe, but I've put it here in **ENTERTAINING** because I don't consider scallops to be an **EVERYDAY** ingredient. This is an easy, impressive starter which you can get ahead with by frying the onions up to 3 days in advance.

Put the butter, onions, fine salt and 3 tablespoons of the oil into a large, non-stick sauté pan on a medium heat. Cook for about 22 minutes, stirring often, until soft and deeply golden-brown. You're after a slow, deep caramelisation here, so don't be tempted to turn the heat up to speed up that process. If the onions are burning or becoming crispy, lower the heat.

Remove from the heat, stir in the curry powder, and set aside.

Rinse the scallops to remove any grit, then pat them dry all over. Put them into a bowl with the oil, fine salt and plenty of black pepper and gently mix to coat.

Lightly grease a large, non-stick frying pan with oil and place on a medium-high heat. Once hot, place the scallops in the pan, spaced apart. Fry for 3 minutes, pressing them down with a spatula, until the undersides have a deep, golden-brown crust. Flip and fry for another 2 minutes on the other side. Transfer to a plate, with the browner side facing up.

Add the remaining 2 tablespoons of oil to the onions (gently warm the onions first if they've been refrigerated or if the oil and butter have set).

Transfer the scallops to a platter and spoon over the onions and oil. If you like heat, use a fine microplane to grate over some dried habanero. Squeeze over plenty of lime juice and serve.

Serves 4

2 aubergines, cut into 3cm pieces (500g)

4 tablespoons olive oil

350g paccheri pasta tubes

2 ripe tomatoes (240g)

1 tablespoon fresh parsley, very
    finely chopped

10g fresh basil leaves

about 20 twists of black pepper

1 lemon, cut into wedges, to serve

fine salt

Confit squid

700g squid, tubes and tentacles,
    cleaned (500g)

200g olive oil

150g sweet, ripe cherry tomatoes,
    such as Datterini

10g fresh basil

5g fresh oregano

4 large cloves of garlic, skin on and
    crushed with the side of a knife

3 tablespoons lemon juice

1 tablespoon tomato purée/paste

½ teaspoon chilli flakes

1 teaspoon Calabrian chilli paste
    aka crema di pepperoncino
    (optional, alternatively use more
    chilli flakes to taste)

1 teaspoon fine salt

Notes

The leftover confit oil can be kept in
the fridge for up to 3 days – use it to
cook fried rice (page 193), to drizzle
over pasta or toast, or to make aïoli.

Confit squid and aubergine paccheri

When I was about eleven, my family went to visit the Pasetti, a wine-producing family my dad works with in Abruzzo, to the east of Rome. Their winery – Contesa – makes brilliant Montepulciano d'Abruzzo and Pecorino d'Abruzzo wines (the latter of which I would highly recommend to go with this dish). One sunny lunch on the terrace, Patrizia Pasetti brought out an unforgettable dish of *pacherri* (large pasta tubes) with a sauce made from grilled squid, aubergines and tomatoes. I've thought about that pasta on and off for twenty years, and it's etched in my memory as one of the greatest things I've ever eaten. This recipe pays homage to that pasta dish, the flavours of which I've tried to recreate as best as I can from memory. In this version I've chosen to confit the squid, as that's my favourite way to cook squid, although Patrizia's was grilled.

If you can't get hold of squid, use prawns or chunks of fish instead. For a vegetarian version, try swapping the squid for oyster mushrooms and cooking them in exactly the same way.

The confit squid is also great on toast, with an aioli made from the confit oil.

———————

Preheat the oven to 210°C fan/230°C.

First make the confit squid. Slice the squid tubes into 2cm-thick rings and place in a large saucepan with the tentacles and all the remaining ingredients for the confit squid. Stir together, then place on the lowest heat possible and cook for 40 minutes, until the squid is very soft – you don't want the oil to get too hot, so every time it starts to bubble, take it off the heat for a few minutes, then return it. After 40 minutes, remove from the heat and leave the squid to cool in the oil while you prepare the rest.

While the squid is cooking, roast the aubergines. Line a large flat baking tray with parchment. Mix the aubergines together with the oil and 1 teaspoon of fine salt and spread out across the tray. Roast for 20 minutes, then stir and roast for another 10 minutes, or until deeply golden-brown.

Drain the squid and confit tomatoes through a sieve set over a bowl to catch the oil. Discard the cooked herbs and garlic skin. Place the squid and confit tomatoes in a large sauté pan along with the roasted aubergines and 150g of the confit oil. Set the pan aside, off the heat.

Continues on next page...

Confit squid and aubergine paccheri continued...

Pour 80g of the remaining confit oil into a medium bowl. Halve the tomatoes and grate the cut sides into the bowl with the oil using the large holes of a box grater. Discard the tomato skin. Add ¼ teaspoon of fine salt and set aside. Pour any remaining oil into a clean jar to use in another recipe (see notes).

Bring a large pot of salted water to the boil, then cook your paccheri until al dente, about 12 minutes. Drain, reserving 50g of the pasta water.

Place the pan with the squid on a medium-high heat, then add the cooked pasta and pasta water. Cook for 5 minutes, tossing every now and then, until the liquid has thickened and coats the pasta. Turn the heat all the way down, then add the grated tomato mixture, along with the parsley, half the basil and plenty of black pepper. Stir together then remove from the heat.

Transfer to a platter or serve from the pan, finishing with the remaining basil and plenty of pepper. Serve with lemon wedges alongside.

1 litre sunflower oil, for frying

hot sauce (optional, if not making
the salsa), to serve

2 limes, cut into wedges, to serve

Croquette filling

40g unsalted butter

60g plain flour

250g whole milk

60g Kewpie mayonnaise
(or another mayo)

250g cooked peeled king prawns, roughly
chopped into 1–2cm pieces

1 clove of garlic, finely grated/crushed

1 jalapeño, finely chopped (deseeded
if you prefer less heat)

10g fresh chives, finely chopped

¾ teaspoon medium curry powder

1 teaspoon finely grated lime zest

1 teaspoon finely grated lemon zest

½ teaspoon fine salt

freshly ground black pepper

Croquette coating

40g plain flour

70g panko breadcrumbs, large
pieces crushed with your hands

1 egg, whisked with ½ tablespoon water

**Tomato and Scotch
bonnet salsa (optional)**

200g sweet, ripe cherry tomatoes,
such as Datterini

1 lime: 1 teaspoon finely grated zest
and 1 tablespoon juice

1½ tablespoons olive oil

¾ teaspoon flaked salt

1–2 Scotch bonnet chillies (or a milder
chilli if you prefer)

Curried prawn and jalapeño croquettes with Scotch bonnet salsa

Croquettes are a little tricky, a little messy, and let's face it, this method might seem dauntingly long. Honestly, I considered not including it in the book because of its length, but I *just had to*, because these are tear-jerkingly delicious, and besides, there are lots of things you can do to prepare ahead and make the whole process more manageable. You can make and portion the mixture up to 2 days before, or indeed you can take them right up to the point where they are panko'd up to a day before, bringing them back to room temperature before frying. In both cases, keep them well covered and refrigerated. The salsa (although optional) can (and should!) be made up to a week ahead and left in the fridge to get a little funky.

———————

For the croquettes, melt the butter in a medium saucepan on a medium heat, then stir in the flour with a whisk until the mixture thickens into a playdough-like paste. Continue cooking for 30 seconds, moving the thick paste around the pan, then lower the heat all the way down and pour in the milk. Whisk vigorously for 1 minute, or until thickened into a completely smooth, thick paste that comes away from the sides of the pan. Remove from the heat and fold in the mayo, prawns, garlic, jalapeño, chives, curry powder, lime zest, lemon zest, fine salt and plenty of black pepper until combined.

Prepare a flat tray that will fit into your fridge. Use 2 dessert spoons to portion the mixture into 12 pieces weighing around 55g each and arrange on the tray, spread apart. It doesn't matter what shape they are for now. Cover with parchment paper and refrigerate for 2 hours, or up to 2 days.

For the salsa (if you're making it), finely chop the cherry tomatoes into very small pieces. Transfer to a medium bowl, using your hands as a natural sieve so you don't take all the liquid and seeds with you (otherwise the salsa will be quite soggy). Stir in the lime zest, lime juice, oil and flaked salt.

Very finely chop the Scotch bonnet – they vary substantially in heat level, so start with ¼ chilli, removing the seeds and pith if you prefer milder heat. Add to the salsa, stir and taste, then add up to 2 finely chopped chillies, to taste.

Prepare your coating work station. Place the flour in one container, the panko in another, and the egg in a third separate container.

Continues on next page...

Prawn croquettes continued...

Line a tray with non-stick parchment paper.

Remove the tray of portioned mixture from the fridge. A few at a time, add the portions to the container of flour. Toss and roll so they're completely coated in flour (if the croquettes aren't completely covered in flour, the filling can leak into the oil as you fry, so be diligent here). Once coated in flour, use your hands to shape each croquette into a ball or cylinder – whatever you prefer, but balls are easiest. If this process creates any surface cracks, roll in flour again. Place on the parchment-lined tray, spaced apart. Continue with the rest until all the croquettes are coated with flour and shaped.

Fill a large sauté pan with the frying oil and place on a medium heat to get to frying temperature. If you're coating the croquettes in advance to get ahead, heat the oil whenever you're ready to start frying.

Next, coat the croquettes in egg and then in panko before returning them to the lined tray. Stick to using one hand for egg and one hand for panko, to avoid having to wash your hands multiple times throughout. One at a time, place a croquette in the egg mixture and use one hand to roll it so it's completely covered in egg. Lower into the container with the panko, then use your other hand to roll the croquette so it's completely covered. Again, be diligent here and roll the croquette enough times to ensure it's completely covered in panko.

Once all the croquettes are coated, check the oil is hot enough to start frying. Drop a piece of panko into the oil and if it sizzles and floats straight to the top, you're ready to go. If you have a temperature probe, the oil should be at 180°C.

Line a tray with absorbent kitchen paper.

Fry the croquettes 4 at a time. Use a slotted spoon to carefully lower the croquettes into the oil, then fry for 2½–4 minutes, turning throughout, until golden-brown all over. If the croquettes are browning very quickly, turn the heat all the way down. Transfer to the paper-lined plate and sprinkle with flaked salt. Continue frying the remaining croquettes, adjusting the heat as you go if necessary.

Serve hot, with the salsa or hot sauce and lime wedges alongside.

2 mackerel, cleaned, gutted
   and butterflied

olive oil

fine salt

green ends of 2 spring onions, thinly
   sliced into rounds

Corn and Calabrian chilli salsa

2 ripe tomatoes (250g)

2 teaspoons Calabrian chilli paste
   aka crema di pepperoncino (use
   very finely chopped red chillies
   or Scotch bonnet as an alternative)

1 large clove of garlic, very finely
   chopped (5g)

¾ teaspoon caster sugar

3 tablespoons olive oil

2 limes: ½ tablespoon juice and the
   rest cut into wedges, to serve

100g frozen corn, defrosted and
   patted dry

fine salt

Notes

I love this salsa with raw fish, as well as grilled. To make a crudo (see plate in the background of the photo), select an extremely fresh, firm fillet of fish (about 60g per person), cut it into cubes or slices, and season with a pinch of salt, a drizzle of good olive oil and a dash of lemon or lime juice (not too much, or the acid will 'cook' the fish). Arrange the salsa on a plate and top with the seasoned fish and spring onions. Finish with a drizzle of really good olive oil and a sprinkle of flaked salt. Serve with lemon or lime wedges. Raw prawns or scallops would also work very well.

Mackerel with charred corn and Calabrian chilli salsa

I love mackerel for its deliciously strong flavour, and also because it's very easy to cook – especially when butterflied. Rather than overcomplicating things by attempting to explain in writing how to butterfly mackerel, I suggest you look up a video online, or better yet, ask your fishmonger to do it for you and watch closely so you can do it yourself next time.

———————

First, make the salsa. Halve the tomatoes and grate the cut sides using the large holes of a box grater. Place the pulp in a sieve set over a bowl and leave to drain for a few minutes. Discard the tomato skins.

Put the drained tomato pulp into a heatproof bowl with 1 tablespoon of the drained tomato juice. Add the Calabrian chilli paste, garlic and sugar and mix well.

Heat the 3 tablespoons of oil in a small saucepan on a medium heat for 1½ minutes, then pour the hot oil into the bowl with the tomato and chilli. Add the lime juice and salt to taste, stir and set aside.

Heat a non-stick frying pan on a high heat. Once the pan is very hot, add the corn, 1 teaspoon of oil and ¼ teaspoon of fine salt. Stir together, then cook for 6 minutes or until the kernels are nicely charred all over, stirring once or twice. Roughly chop the corn and stir into the salsa.

Preheat the oven grill to the highest setting.

Pat the butterflied mackerel dry on both sides (the drier the skin, the more it will char). Add to a bowl, season generously with oil and fine salt and carefully rub to coat both sides.

Place the butterflied mackerel on a flat baking tray, skin side up. Grill on the top shelf of the oven for 6 minutes, or until the skin has bubbled and slightly charred (keep an eye on the oven; all grills are different so this could take more or less time). If you have a blowtorch, use it on the skin side to char it further.

Spoon the salsa onto a platter and top with the spring onions. Place the mackerel on top, skin side up. Sprinkle with flaked salt, squeeze over some lime and serve.

250g fresh lasagne sheets

130g double cream, plus
      2 tablespoons to serve

100g Parmesan, finely grated

10g fresh chives, finely chopped

Prawn ragù

6 tablespoons olive oil

½ onion, finely chopped

5 cloves of garlic, finely grated/crushed

200g sweet, ripe cherry tomatoes,
      such as Datterini, finely chopped

1 teaspoon fine salt

500g raw peeled king prawns,
      very finely chopped to mince
      consistency (about 1kg if you're
      starting with shell-on prawns –
      use the shells to make a stock)

1 dried habanero chilli (or chilli flakes
      if you prefer less heat)

80g tomato purée/paste

2 teaspoons white miso paste

about 50 twists of freshly ground
      black pepper

100g white wine

500g fish, shellfish or chicken stock
      (unsalted liquid stock, not cubes)

Habanero oil

120g olive oil

2 teaspoons tomato purée/paste

½ teaspoon chipotle flakes

1 dried habanero chilli, seeds
      discarded, finely chopped
      (use less habanero or a pinch of
      regular chilli flakes if you prefer)

½ teaspoon sweet paprika

¼ teaspoon fine salt

Prawn lasagne with habanero oil

This recipe is very close to my heart, and as with many of my favourite recipes, I've tweaked it more times than I could count on two hands. In its first incarnation, I started with shell-on prawns, making a stock from the shells and an oil laced with habanero with the fried prawn heads. Rather than a béchamel, I made a homemade version of Catupiry, a Brazilian cheese spread which is hard to describe and really needs to be tasted to be understood, because it tastes nothing like regular cheese spread.

This lasagne is the purest representation of me; a homage to the countries that have shaped me as a person and a cook. In its original form it was one part Italian (the pasta), one part Mexican (the habanero) and one part Brazilian (the Catupiry). This particular version is simplified, no Catupiry and no prawn head oil, but I hope you'll agree that it's still magical.

For the ragù, put 4 tablespoons of the oil into a large sauté pan on a medium heat with the onion, garlic, cherry tomatoes and fine salt. Fry, stirring often, for 8–10 minutes or until the onions are soft and golden and the tomatoes have broken down.

Increase the heat to high, add the chopped prawns and fry for another 8 minutes, stirring every now and then, until the prawn mince has taken on some colour.

Add the habanero (or chilli flakes), tomato purée/paste, miso and plenty of pepper. Continue to fry for 3 minutes, stirring every now and then. Turn the heat down if the mixture starts to catch or burn.

Pour over the wine and let it bubble away for 30 seconds. Add the stock (or water) and the remaining 2 tablespoons of oil, bring to a simmer, then reduce the heat to medium-low and simmer gently for about 18–20 minutes. Remove the habanero, squeezing it into the sauce first if you like heat.

Meanwhile, put all the ingredients for the habanero oil into a small saucepan and place on a medium heat. Whisk just to incorporate the tomato paste, then heat until gently bubbling, about 1½ minutes. Remove from the heat and set aside. Once cool, transfer to a clean jar (you won't use it all for this recipe).

Continues on next page...

Prawn lasagne continued...

Preheat the oven to 200°C fan/220°C.

To assemble, cover the bottom of a small baking dish (about 20 x 20cm or a similar size) with lasagne sheets, then spread over a fifth of the ragù. Follow with a fifth each of the cream, Parmesan and chives. Continue layering in the same way until you've used up all the ingredients. Drizzle over ½ tablespoon of the habanero oil, cover tightly with foil and bake for 20 minutes.

Increase the oven heat to 230°C fan/250°C, remove the foil and bake for another 10–12 minutes, or until the edges are crisp.

Leave to cool for 10 minutes. Finish with the remaining 2 tablespoons of cream and a good drizzle of the habanero oil, and serve.

Notes

I love habanero, but it's extremely hot, and you may not. You can decrease the habanero if you like, or sub with a pinch of chilli flakes (you'll know best how much you can handle) for milder heat.

Make ahead

The ragù can be made up to 2 days before and kept refrigerated. The habanero oil will keep for up to 3 weeks in the fridge.

MEAT

Serves 4 as a starter or 2 as a main

2 x 170g skin-on duck breasts (340g)

fine salt

1 lime, cut into wedges, to serve

Marinade

2 tablespoons soy sauce

1¼ tablespoons Worcestershire sauce

½ tablespoon maple syrup

⅛ teaspoon fine salt

Spring onion salsa

2 spring onions, very finely
    chopped (25g)

5g fresh chives, very finely chopped

5g fresh ginger, peeled and
    very finely chopped

½ jalapeño, very finely chopped

3 tablespoons olive oil

1 teaspoon lime juice

⅛ teaspoon fine salt

Mexicorn sauce

1 tablespoon unsalted butter (15g)

1½ tablespoons olive oil

1 banana shallot, very finely
    chopped (30g)

1 clove of garlic, very finely chopped

⅛ teaspoon fine salt

½ teaspoon freshly ground black pepper

2 teaspoons green peppercorns,
    roughly crushed (use pickled green
    peppercorns if you can find them)

¼ teaspoon chipotle chilli flakes
    (or more if not using habanero)

1 dried habanero chilli (optional)

1¼ teaspoons ground cumin

2 tablespoons water

130g single cream

Duck with Mexicorn sauce and spring onion salsa

Duck with peppercorn sauce is one of my all-time favourite combinations, but of course I couldn't just give you a classic recipe for duck with peppercorn sauce because, well, what on earth would be the point of that? In true **MEZCLA** style, this peppercorn sauce is laced with cumin, chipotle and habanero. It's a Mexicorn sauce, if you will. Purists, look away now, this peppercorn sauce is pure, brazen fusion, containing both Worcestershire and soy sauce, as well as chilli and spices.

Mix the marinade ingredients together in a container big enough to fit both duck breasts in a single layer. Arrange the breasts in the marinade, skin side up. Try to make sure that the skin is not touching the marinade – the drier the skin remains, the crispier it will eventually be. Marinate for at least 2 hours at room temperature, or preferably overnight, refrigerated. Don't cover the container with the lid in either instance, you want the skin to air-dry. Bring to room temperature 2 hours before cooking.

For the salsa, mix all the ingredients together and set aside.

Remove the duck breasts from the marinade. Set the marinade aside to use later. Transfer the breasts to a tray lined with a clean absorbent cloth, flesh side down, so the flesh dries out. Blot the skin with kitchen paper to ensure it's as dry as possible. Rub a good pinch of salt and plenty of pepper into the skin of each breast.

In a cold, non-stick frying pan off the heat, place the room-temperature duck breasts skin side down and spaced apart. Place the pan on the lowest heat and gently fry – pressing down on the breasts so they colour evenly – for 9–10 minutes or until the skin is crisp and a deep, golden-brown. Spoon away any fat that renders in the pan as the breasts cooks. Transfer the duck breasts to a plate, skin side up. Increase the heat to high.

Once the pan is very hot, return the breasts to the pan, this time flesh side down and set a stopwatch. Once the underside has taken on a nice golden-brown colour, use tongs to keep moving the flesh side of the breasts around the pan, using the sides of the pan as support – the aim is for all sides of the flesh to be coloured evenly. This should take 2½–3 minutes for rare or 4 minutes for medium-rare.

Continues on next page...

Duck with Mexicorn sauce continued...

Transfer to a plate skin side up and leave to rest, uncovered, for 12 minutes (this long rest is important). Wash the pan thoroughly and let it cool down before making the sauce (or use another pan).

For the Mexicorn sauce, add the butter, oil, shallots, garlic and salt to the cleaned and cooled non-stick frying pan. Place on a medium-low heat and very gently fry for 6–7 minutes, stirring often until the onion is soft and golden, then add the black pepper, the peppercorns, the chipotle, habanero and cumin and cook for 1 minute more.

Pour the reserved marinade and the water into the pan, increase the heat to high and leave to bubble away for 1½ minutes. Reduce the heat to low then stir in the cream and cook for 1 more minute. At this point, squeeze the habanero with the back of a spoon to release its flavour before removing it, or remove it without squeezing it if you prefer subtle heat.

Pour the sauce on to a platter or individual plates. Slice the duck breasts and arrange on top of the sauce. Finish with some of the spring onion salsa and serve with lime wedges on the side.

Notes

Oyster mushroom skewers are a great alternative to duck if you want to keep this dish vegetarian. Marinate your mushrooms in olive oil and salt, and roast them as per the method on page 53. The duck marinade ingredients form part of the final Mexicorn sauce, so don't forget them even if you're going veg.

Make ahead

Marinate the duck up to 2 days ahead, ensuring the skin isn't in contact with the marinade. Keep refrigerated without a lid so the skin air-dries.

3 x 180g pork shoulder steaks,
    2cm thick (540g)

3 tablespoons mild and light olive oil

2 mild red chillies, thinly sliced
    into rounds and deseeded

5g fresh Thai basil leaves

lime wedges, to serve

Marinade

4 cloves of garlic, roughly chopped

10g fresh ginger, peeled
    and roughly chopped

1 tablespoon black peppercorns,
    roughly crushed

80g soy sauce

1½ teaspoons Worcestershire sauce

60g maple syrup

5g fresh lime leaves or lemongrass,
    roughly chopped

Grilled pineapple and veg

½ very ripe pineapple, peeled, cored
    and cut into 2½cm-thick wedges

120g small green peppers (Padrón,
    friggitelli or Turkish), halved if large

6 spring onions (100g)

½ large onion, finely sliced and
    rings separated

1 tablespoon maple syrup

2 tablespoons olive oil

½ teaspoon salt

Black pepper pork steaks with pineapple and peppers

Pork shoulder is an incredibly flavourful and forgiving cut of meat with lots of marbling (avoid loin steaks at all costs, they have little to no intramuscular fat). A cast iron skillet is the best pan for the job here, as it will help you get a really good golden-brown crust on your steaks. Having said that, the marinade can make the pan very smoky, so if you can barbecue outside, that's even better. Make sure your pineapple is very ripe, soft and sweet – it will make all the difference.

––––––––––

Put all the ingredients for the marinade into a container, mix, then add the steaks. Leave to marinate for at least 30 minutes, and preferably overnight, turning a few times so both sides are evenly marinated.

When you're 30 minutes away from being ready to serve, remove the steaks from the marinade and transfer to a plate lined with kitchen paper. Pick off all the aromatics stuck to the steaks. Pat both sides of the steaks dry and set aside.

Strain the marinade into a medium saucepan, discarding the aromatics. Add 50g of water to the marinade and set aside for later.

Turn the oven to the highest grill setting. Place all the ingredients for the grilled pineapple and veg on a flat, sturdy baking tray and mix so everything is coated in maple syrup, oil and salt. Grill on the top shelf of the oven for about 8 minutes or until the vegetables are nicely charred (all grills are different so this may take more or less time). If you have a blowtorch, use it to get a better char on the pineapple. Alternatively you can grill everything on a griddle pan or a barbecue, until nicely charred on both sides. Turn the grill off and keep the pineapple and veg warm in the oven.

Prepare a heatproof sieve set over a heatproof bowl. Heat the 3 tablespoons of oil in a small, non-stick frying pan. Once very hot, add the chillies and fry for about 1 minute and 40 seconds, swirling the pan to separate the slices, then add the Thai basil and fry for another 20–30 seconds, until crisp. Strain through the sieve over the bowl to collect the aromatic oil.

Continues on next page...

Make ahead

Marinate the pork up to 2 days ahead and keep refrigerated. Bring to room temperature before cooking.

Black pepper pork steaks continued...

Place a large, seasoned cast-iron pan (or a large, non-stick frying pan) on a high heat. Open the windows and turn on the extractor fan.

Once the pan is very hot, brush both sides of the steaks with some of the aromatic oil. Place in the very hot pan – if the meat doesn't sizzle immediately, the pan isn't hot enough. Fry for 2½ minutes on the first side, pressing the steaks down with a spatula until you get a good, golden-brown crust. Flip and cook for another 1½ minutes on the other side, pressing down again to get a good char. Flip and cook for another 1 minute on that side, then flip and cook for another 1 minute. Transfer to a board or plate to rest for 8 minutes, flipping halfway.

Place the pan with the marinade and water on a medium heat. Cook for 5 minutes until hot and slightly reduced, then remove from the heat.

Arrange the grilled pineapple and veg on a platter. Slice the rested pork and arrange on top. Spoon over the hot marinade, then squeeze over some lime wedges. Drizzle over some of the reserved aromatic oil. Top with the crispy chilli and basil, finish with plenty of pepper and serve.

2 x 280g lamb loin fillets, with the
    fat on (560g) (see intro)
½ teaspoon fine salt
½ teaspoon Urfa chilli flakes

Miso butter

45g ghee (from a jar not a tin, see page 17)
    or unsalted butter
2 tablespoons olive oil
10g white miso paste
1 large clove of garlic, finely
    chopped (not crushed)
5g fresh sage leaves
3 strips of lemon peel
about 30 twists of freshly ground
    black pepper
⅛ teaspoon fine salt

Ajvar

1 medium aubergine, halved
    lengthways (270g)
6 red romano peppers, left whole (780g)
1 clove of garlic, finely grated/crushed
1½ teaspoon pul biber or Aleppo
    chilli flakes
2 teaspoons lemon juice (save the
    rest of the lemon, to serve)
¾ teaspoon fine salt
5g fresh mint leaves, finely chopped

Make ahead

Marinate the lamb up to 2 days ahead
and keep refrigerated. Bring back to room
temperature before cooking. The ajvar will
keep for up to 2 weeks in the fridge.

Lamb loin fillets with ajvar and miso butter

Make sure you get loin fillets with the fat on. You might have to go to your butcher for this, but cooking the lamb fat side down slowly, starting in a cold pan, creates the most perfect crispy-yet-soft layer of fat and you really don't want to miss out on that.

Ajvar is a condiment traditionally made in the Balkans region of south-east Europe using roasted peppers and aubergines. It's one of my favourite condiments to have on hand to add to pretty much anything savoury – from eggs to toast to roast chicken. If you're making the ajvar without the lamb, add some olive oil and extra salt to the mix, as you won't be serving it with the miso butter.

———

Preheat the oven to 230°C fan/250°C.

Put all the ingredients for the miso butter into a medium saucepan. Mix to incorporate the miso and garlic, then place on a medium-low heat and cook for 2½ minutes, until gently bubbling. Leave to cool for a few minutes.

Pat the lamb fillets dry. In a small bowl, mix together ½ teaspoon of fine salt, ½ teaspoon of Urfa chilli flakes and 1½ tablespoons of the cooled miso butter (avoiding the solids). Rub this mixture all over the lamb and set aside to marinate while you roast the vegetables.

Cut deep cross-hatches into the flesh side of the aubergine halves and place on a flat baking tray, cut side up, along with the whole peppers. Roast for 25 minutes, turning everything over halfway, until the aubergines are very soft, and the peppers are blackened. Remove from the oven.

Turn the oven down to 160°C fan/180°C.

When cool enough to handle, peel and deseed the peppers and transfer the flesh to a chopping board. Scoop the cooked flesh of the aubergines on to the peppers, discarding the skin. Add the garlic, pul biber, lemon juice and fine salt and chop everything into a rough mash with a large knife. Set aside.

Off the heat, place the lamb fillets fat side down in an unheated cast-iron pan (or a non-stick frying pan). Place on a medium heat, then place a smaller pan on top of the fillets to weigh them down.

Continues on next page...

Lamb loin fillets continued...

Slowly fry for 8 minutes, or until the fat side is deeply golden-brown and crisp. Flip the fillets and cook for 1 minute on the flesh side, turning so all sides of the flesh make contact with the pan. Place the lamb on a flat baking tray, fat side up, and transfer to the oven for 6 minutes to cook through. Rest on a chopping board, fat side up, for 10 minutes. Don't skip the rest – this part is really important.

Once the lamb has rested, return the pan with the miso butter to a medium heat and gently cook until melted.

Mix the mint with the ajvar and spoon on to a platter. Slice the lamb, sprinkle with flaked salt and arrange on top. Spoon the miso butter over the lamb and ajvar. Finish with Urfa chilli, squeeze over some lemon juice and serve.

Roast chicken curry with crispy curry leaves

1 spatchcocked chicken (about 1.7kg),
    at room temperature

3 tablespoons olive oil

2 red chillies, thinly sliced into rounds

30 fresh curry leaves

fine salt

Marinade

60g mayonnaise

2 tablespoons olive oil

1 tablespoon medium curry powder

¼ teaspoon cayenne or Kashmiri
    chilli powder

1 teaspoon fine salt

Curry sauce

400g tin of full-fat coconut milk (at least
    70% coconut extract)

1 tablespoon tomato purée/paste

15g fresh ginger, peeled and
    roughly chopped

100g sweet, ripe cherry tomatoes,
    such as Datterini

½ onion, roughly chopped

¼ teaspoon cayenne or Kashmiri
    chilli powder

1½ tablespoons medium curry powder

½ teaspoon ground turmeric

1 tablespoon maple syrup

150g water

1¼ teaspoons fine salt

Notes

To check if it's cooked, insert a metal skewer
into the thickest part of the chicken; if the
juices run clear, you're good to go.

Use any leftover chicken to make
Cannelloni enchiladas, page 225.

Make ahead

Marinate the chicken up to 2 days ahead
and keep refrigerated. Bring back to room
temperature before roasting.

The chicken roasts over the curry sauce, all in the same tray at the same time, enriching the curry with its fat and juices as it cooks. You might rightly wonder why there's mayonnaise in the marinade, but trust me on this one, it keeps the flesh moist and the skin crispy. Don't ask me how, just enjoy the magic.

The chicken here is spatchcocked, which is my favourite way to roast chicken. Rather than trying to explain how to do that in words (or with pictures of a spreadeagled raw chicken), I suggest that you look on YouTube or on my Instagram highlights for a tutorial, because it's much easier to learn by watching it being done. Alternatively, ask your butcher to do it for you, and watch closely so you can do it yourself next time.

The size of the roasting tray (32 x 26cm) is important here. If your tray is larger, keep an eye on the curry sauce as it roasts, adding water to the sauce, if needed, to stop it burning around the edges.

———

Preheat the oven to 230°C fan/250°C. In a small bowl, mix all the ingredients for the marinade. Pat the chicken dry with paper towels. Sprinkle all over with fine salt, including the underside. Slather the marinade all over and around the chicken. Leave to marinate for at least 30 minutes, or up to overnight, refrigerated (in which case bring back to room temperature before roasting).

Place all the ingredients for the curry sauce in a blender and blitz until smooth. Pour into a 32 x 26cm high-sided roasting tray (see recipe introduction about tray size). Place the chicken in the tray skin-side up on top of the curry sauce, making sure its legs are spread out so the skin can brown and crisp up evenly.

Roast for 40 minutes (without basting), until the chicken is cooked through and crispy and the sauce has thickened and is bubbling. Leave to rest for 15 minutes.

While the chicken is resting, put the 3 tablespoons of olive oil into a small saucepan on a medium-high heat. Once hot, add the chillies and fry for 2 minutes, then add the curry leaves and fry for 30 seconds. Drain through a heatproof sieve into a heatproof bowl. You won't need the frying oil, but keep it to drizzle over another dish.

Transfer the chicken to a lipped platter and pour the curry sauce around it (or just serve the chicken and sauce directly from the tray). Top with the crispy chilli and curry leaves and serve.

Serves 4

350g leftover roast chicken, finely chopped (see intro)

2 tablespoons lime juice

½ teaspoon fine salt

8 fresh lasagne sheets

lime wedges, to serve

Cumin béchamel

40g unsalted butter

40g plain flour

450g whole milk

1 clove of garlic, finely grated/crushed

1½ teaspoons ground cumin

½ teaspoon chipotle flakes

100g mozzarella, drained and chopped

1 teaspoon fine salt

Salsa roja

250g chicken stock (or water)

200g tomato passata

30g tomato purée/paste

2 cloves of garlic, finely grated/crushed

15g butter, melted

1 teaspoon ground cumin

½ teaspoon dried Mexican (or regular) oregano

1 teaspoon chipotle flakes

½ teaspoon fine salt

Salsa fresca

1 medium, ripe tomato, finely chopped (100g)

1 red chilli, finely chopped

¼ onion, finely chopped (30g)

20g olive oil, plus extra to serve

20g lime juice

¼ teaspoon fine salt

5g fresh coriander, finely chopped

Notes

Use marinated tofu instead of chicken for a vegetarian version. To make this vegan, use dairy-free alternatives, and dried lasagne instead of fresh lasagne). Dried lasagne sheets will need to be boiled before using.

Cannelloni enchiladas

This recipe is a classic example of one of my favourite *mezclas* – that is, the *mezcla* of Italian and Mexican cuisine. Here béchamel, mozzarella and pasta come together with cumin, chipotle and coriander in a union that makes all the sense in the world when you taste it.

This recipe was created as a way to use up leftover chicken from the Roast chicken curry on page 222. If you don't have leftover chicken, use shop-bought rotisserie chicken or roast a chicken before starting this recipe.

Mix the chicken with the lime and salt and set aside.

For the béchamel, melt the butter in a medium saucepan on a medium heat. Once melted, whisk in the flour to get a smooth, thick paste. Cook for 1 minute, whisking continuously, then slowly pour in the milk, whisking vigorously to get rid of any lumps. Cook for 1½ minutes (keep whisking!) or until the mixture has thickened to a smooth béchamel.

Remove from the heat and add the garlic, cumin, chipotle, mozzarella and fine salt. Stir until the mozzarella has melted with the residual heat. Transfer half the béchamel to a separate container and set aside to use later. Stir the chicken into the remaining béchamel in the pan. Set aside.

Put all the ingredients for the salsa roja into a bowl and whisk until combined. Pour two-thirds of the salsa into a 32 x 24cm baking dish.

Preheat the oven to 180°C fan/200°C.

Place the lasagne sheets in a large heatproof container, cover with boiling water and leave to soften for a few minutes.

One sheet at a time, take the lasagne out of the water and place on a work surface. If your lasagne sheets are around A5 size, have the shorter edge facing you. If they're much smaller, have the longer edge facing you.

Continues on next page...

Cannelloni enchiladas continued...

Arrange about 75g of the chicken mix along the edge closest to you, then tightly roll up and place in the tray, seam side down. Continue with the rest until you've filled the tray. Pour over the rest of the salsa roja, followed by the remaining béchamel. Drizzle with some olive oil, then bake for 30 minutes.

Meanwhile, for the salsa fresca, mix together the tomatoes, chilli, onion, oil, lime juice and salt.

When you're ready to serve, stir the coriander into the salsa fresca. Top the hot cannelloni with the salsa fresca, drizzle with some more olive oil and serve with extra lime wedges on the side.

4 x bone-in individual short ribs (2kg)

2 tablespoons sunflower oil

2 onions, halved and thinly sliced

6 cloves of garlic, crushed with
the side of a knife

2 tomatoes, finely chopped (240g)

1 teaspoon fine salt

2 tablespoons red pepper paste
(or tomato purée/paste)

2 tablespoons Worcestershire sauce

1 litre chicken or beef bone broth/stock
(you can sub some of this with water,
if you like)

200g pure pomegranate juice

80g watercress

Mole rub

2 dried ancho chillies, stalks removed,
torn in half

1 dried cascabel chilli, stalk removed,
torn in half

1 dried whole chipotle chilli, stalk and
seeds removed, torn in half

4 cinnamon sticks, roughly broken

1 tablespoon cocoa powder

2 teaspoons black peppercorns,
roughly crushed

1 tablespoon fine salt

Notes

I use a mix of ancho, chipotle and
cascabel chillies in my rub, but feel free
to experiment with whatever dried chillies
you have to hand (although I'd advise
sticking to those with mild/medium heat).

Mole short ribs com agrião

This is inspired by two of my favourite dishes – Mexican mole and a Brazilian dish called *rabada com agrião*. This version is (of course) not a traditional version of either of these dishes.

Mole is from the Nahuatl word 'mõlli', meaning sauce, and it's a word I've always been drawn to, because my name also comes from Nahuatl (the language spoken by most Mexicans at the time of the Spanish conquest). There are countless variations of mole, but most contain a blend of dried chillies, chocolate and spices, with either nuts, seeds or corn tortillas to thicken. This version doesn't contain any of the traditional thickeners, but the flavour profile is very much inspired by mole.

Rabada com agrião is a Brazilian oxtail and watercress stew that features onions, garlic and tomatoes as a base, with watercress stirred through towards the end. This version uses short ribs instead of oxtail, simply because you get more meat for your money. The result is impossibly soft, fall-apart meat in a rich, sweet, spiced and slightly chocolatey sauce, with watercress to cut through the richness. Serve with the cassava gratin on page 164 and/or the curried cornbread on page 153. It's also great with soft polenta, mashed potatoes or corn tortillas. Use any leftover meat to make ragù or lasagne.

Put all the ingredients for the rub into a blender or mortar and blitz or pound to get a coarse powder.

With a very sharp knife, remove the layer of fat and silver skin over the meaty side of the ribs (not the bone side). You might want to ask your butcher to do this, if that's an option. Pat the ribs dry and place them on a tray. Rub each rib all over with 1 tablespoon of the mole rub (4 tablespoons in total).

Place a large, heavy-bottomed casserole pan (for which you have a lid) on a high heat and add the oil. Turn on the extractor fan. Once very hot, add all the ribs to the pan (or as many as you can fit without overcrowding), bone side up. Sear until deeply browned on all 3 of the longer sides (no need to brown the bone side or the 2 shorter ends). This should take 4–5 minutes per side, 12–15 minutes in total. Transfer the ribs to a plate and set aside. Remove the pan from the heat.

Continues on next page...

Mole short ribs continued...

Preheat the oven to 140°C fan/160°C.

Add the onions and garlic to the same pan and return to a medium-high heat. Fry for 7 minutes, stirring often, or until the onions are soft and golden-brown. Add the tomatoes and fine salt and continue to fry for 2 minutes, then add the red pepper (or tomato) paste and Worcestershire sauce and stir-fry for another 1 minute.

Add the stock, pomegranate juice and remaining mole rub and stir together.

Return the ribs to the pan, bone side up. Cover with a lid and transfer to the oven for 4–5 hours, or until the meat is extremely soft and falling off the bone. Every now and then, remove the lid and make sure the meat is submerged and the bone side of the ribs is still facing up, as any meat above the surface of the liquid won't soften. Remove from the oven and leave the ribs to rest in the pan for another 20–30 minutes, with the lid left on.

Transfer the ribs to a tray, then skim away as much fat as possible. Return the pan to the heat until warm, then remove from the heat and stir in the watercress. Return the ribs to the pan and serve.

END

Rather than splitting the desserts between **EVERYDAY** and **ENTERTAINING**, which would be rather confusing, I've grouped them all here, at **THE END**. Fear not, though, this chapter is helpfully divided into desserts that you can get on the table in (next to) no time at all (**QUICK FIXES**), and desserts that might need a little more love and attention (**SHOWSTOPPERS**).

QUICK FIXES are the answer to the insatiable cravings that usually hit around 8pm on a weeknight, or after a big meal. They are all very simple, and most will take you no longer than 20 minutes.

I don't tend to order dessert at a restaurant unless I'm coerced into it; more often than not, I'm just too full. I do enjoy sweet things, but I tend to eat them between meals, rather than after them. After a big meal, I'd rather just have a quick fix. Something sweet, salty and small, nothing overwhelming, something to scratch an itch without sending me into a state of *abbiocco* (my favourite untranslatable/completely relatable Italian word that vaguely describes the need for a nap after a big meal).

My ultimate quick fixes take just a few minutes to make and are the perfect symphony of sweet and salty (see *Pane, vino e zucchero* and *Romeo e Julieta* page 234).

But this book isn't just about what I like, though, so I've also included a few quick recipes that are proper desserts. Pineapple steaks with maple custard (page 245) features the easiest and quickest custard you'll ever make. Black Forest crumpets (page 236) stars crumpets that are first caramelised in butter and sugar, then topped with cream, Black Forest fruits and chocolate sauce. I guarantee they will be the start of an obsession.

As for **SHOWSTOPPERS**, I'm playing fast and loose with the word. That's to say, some of these recipes are indeed showstopping in the sense that they'll make your jaw drop. Others, however, are showstopping in the sense that you might literally have to stop that show you're watching and concentrate a little more than you would if you were making a recipe from **QUICK FIXES**. They are not necessarily more complicated, they just need more time and attention.

Most of the recipes in **SHOWSTOPPERS** require various elements to set or chill overnight, so be sure to read through the recipe carefully ahead of time and plan accordingly. It's likely that you can make things much easier for yourself by starting some elements a day or two ahead, and then you can calmly and casually whip out your dessert when the time is right.

QUICK FIXES

Pane, vino e zucchero

Serves 4

4 slices of brioche, sourdough or
    focaccia (I like brioche for this)
red wine
demerara sugar

Pane, vino e zucchero (bread with wine and sugar) does what it says on the tin, so to speak, but it's also so much greater than the sum of its parts. My childhood best friend in Italy, Giuditta, introduced me to this snack when I was about four years old, and we often ate it for *merenda* (the afternoon snack you have when you get home from school). Traditionally it's made with unsalted, stale bread, but with all due respect to my beloved Tuscans, there's no sane reason to not add salt to your bread in the 21st century, it's no longer an expensive commodity. Although completely untraditional, I like to use toasted brioche for this snack, but toasted sourdough or focaccia would also work well. As for the wine, it has to be red and it really should be Tuscan, or at the very least Italian. Tuscans would traditionally use caster sugar, but when Giuditta and I made this at my house, we only had access to (crunchy) brown sugar because of my mum's aversion to anything refined, and now that's how I prefer it. If you're not feeling up to making dessert, and you have a few glugs of red wine left after a dinner party, this is the perfect end to a meal.

———

Toast your brioche well in a dry, hot pan. Transfer to a serving plate and douse generously with red wine. Sprinkle over plenty of demerera sugar and enjoy.

Romeo e Julieta

Serves 4

about 150g *goiabada*
    (or membrillo/quince paste)
about 150g cheese, I like to use
    a hard Cheddar-style goats'
    cheese or a young, soft pecorino
extra virgin olive oil
flaked salt

In Brazil, *Romeo e Julieta* not only refers to Shakespeare's star-crossed lovers but also to the combination of cheese with *goiabada* (guava paste). In its simplest form, this is a couple of squares of cheese (usually *queijo Minas*, an unpasteurised cow's cheese from Minas Gerais) and a couple of squares of *goiabada* on a toothpick. The possibilities are endless, however, and you can make anything from cakes, pastries, cheesecakes, pancakes and ice creams based on this combination. I'm keeping things simple here, and just suggesting you serve cheese and *goiabada* together, perhaps with some toast. For me, this is the perfect end to a meal, an unbeatable union of sweet and savoury, a dessert and a cheese course all rolled into one. Untraditionally, I like to finish this with extra virgin olive oil and flaked salt. *Goiabada* is available in any Brazilian shop, but if you can't get hold of it you can use membrillo/quince paste instead. *Queijo minas* might be a little harder to come by outside of Brazil, so sub it with your favourite cheese.

———

Cut the *goiabada* (or membrillo/quince paste) and your chosen cheese into bite-size squares. Skewer onto toothpicks and finish with oil and flaked salt.

Black Forest crumpets

200g frozen Black Forest fruits, defrosted

1 tablespoon caster sugar

2 teaspoons kirsch (optional, or sub with
  regular brandy or another booze)

½ teaspoon tangerine or orange zest

½ teaspoon vanilla bean paste

Caramelised crumpets

60g unsalted butter

4 tablespoons caster sugar

4 crumpets

To serve

150g cooking chocolate (I like to
  use a mix of milk and dark)

120g extra-thick double cream
  (or whipped double cream)

caster sugar

4 cherries, stalks on (optional)

edible gold dust (absolutely optional
  and really quite unnecessary)

Despite being my dream dessert on paper (chocolate, sour fruit, booze, cream), I've never actually tried Black Forest gâteau. With these crumpets, I'm even further away from having tried the real deal (purists, forgive me). This dessert is the definition of a quick fix, in my opinion. The only bit of hands-on cooking is melting butter, and I'm really not even sure that counts.

The caramelised crumpets are a sweet, crunchy revelation. They're also great as sweet croutons to top desserts with, when cut into cubes. Spray them with edible gold dust to make them look like fool's gold – completely unnecessary, but quite fun.

———————

First make sure to defrost the forest fruits.

Preheat the oven to 200°C fan/220°C.

For the crumpets, melt the butter in a small saucepan on a medium heat, then remove from the heat and stir in the sugar. Transfer to a medium bowl with the crumpets and mix to coat them completely. Place the crumpets on a parchment-lined baking tray and bake for 15 minutes, or until crisp, golden-brown and caramelised.

Put the defrosted fruits into a bowl with the sugar, kirsch, tangerine zest and vanilla. Feel free to add more booze, and for a Christmassy version, you could add spices like cinnamon, nutmeg or clove. Roughly crush the fruits with a potato masher or whisk, then mix well.

Put the chocolate into a heatproof bowl and set over a pan of gently simmering water until melted, then leave to cool so it doesn't melt the cream.

Top each crumpet with a quarter of the fruit mix, followed by a large spoonful of cream. Sprinkle the cream with some sugar. Spoon over the chocolate, top with a cherry (and some gold dust if you're feeling extra) and serve.

Make ahead

Prepare the Black Forest fruits up to
2 days ahead and keep refrigerated.

Notes

I like to dust these with cocoa powder,
to offset the sweetness.

Sticky banana and chocolate pan-cake

Chocolate cake

90g unsalted butter

150g milk cooking chocolate,
    roughly chopped

80g dark cooking chocolate,
    roughly chopped

100g soft light brown sugar

40g plain flour

50g ground almonds

40g cocoa powder

¾ teaspoon baking powder

4 eggs, whisked

⅛ teaspoon fine salt

Caramelised bananas

2 tablespoons mild olive oil or sunflower oil

4 small ripe bananas (460g), peeled and
    sliced 1cm thick (340g)

30g unsalted butter, chopped
    into small pieces

3 tablespoons maple syrup, plus
    extra to serve

½ teaspoon vanilla bean paste

½ teaspoon flaked salt, plus extra to serve

Vanilla cream

150g extra-thick double cream
    (or whipped double cream)

½ teaspoon vanilla bean paste

fine salt

Notes

Please don't worry if the banana slices get stuck to the pan once flipped – this is a rustic dessert and you can easily peel the banana slices off the pan and return them to their rightful place on the cake. If you don't have a non-stick, ovenproof frying pan, fry the bananas in whatever pan you have, then carefully transfer them, browned side down, to a lined and greased 23cm cake tin along with the caramel. Spoon the batter on top then bake as normal.

This is a pan-cake (a cake made in a frying pan), not a pancake, which is a semantic difference but quite a big one. Here, a one-bowl chocolate cake batter is spooned over caramelised bananas and finished in the oven. The result is a fondant-like cake with a soft, oozing chocolate centre, topped with sticky bananas. Serve this cake hot from the oven, with cold cream. I like extra-thick double cream here but you might prefer pouring cream. Make sure you use ripe, sweet bananas with plenty of brown spots, or they won't caramelise properly.

————

Preheat the oven to 180°C fan/200°C.

Start the chocolate cake. Place the butter and half each of the chopped milk and dark chocolate in a large heatproof bowl set over a pan of gently simmering water. Cook, stirring, until most of the chocolate has melted. Remove the bowl from the heat. Add all the remaining ingredients for the cake, including the remaining chocolate, but don't mix yet. Set aside.

For the bananas, put the oil into a 28cm medium, non-stick, ovenproof frying pan and place on a medium heat. Once the oil is hot, arrange the banana slices to cover the bottom of the pan and fry for 3 minutes without stirring or flipping.

Increase the heat to medium-high, then distribute the butter, maple syrup, vanilla bean paste and flaked salt evenly over the banana slices. Cook for 6 minutes, swirling the butter and maple syrup around the pan as they form a caramel together. The bananas will soften and caramelise on the bottom, but if you feel they're burning, lower the heat a little. After those 6 minutes are up, remove the pan from the heat.

Mix the cake batter until fully incorporated, then spoon evenly over the bananas. Bake in the top half of the oven for 10 minutes, rotating the pan halfway, until *just* set on top but still quite soft and gooey beneath. Leave to cool for 5 minutes.

Mix the cream with the vanilla and a pinch of salt.

Use a spatula to gently ease the cake away from the sides of the pan. Place a large plate on top of the pan and flip the cake on to it. There's a good chance some of the banana slices will remain stuck to the pan, but you can just peel them off and replace them, browned side up. Sprinkle the cake with flaked salt, then top with the cold vanilla cream. Drizzle over some more maple syrup and serve.

Roasted strawberries

300g ripe strawberries, green tops
    removed, large strawberries
    quartered and smaller ones halved

50g caster sugar

½ lime

2 cinnamon sticks, roughly broken

Whipped yoghurt

150g mascarpone, fridge-cold

200g yoghurt, fridge-cold

½ teaspoon vanilla bean paste

1 tablespoon maple syrup

Peanut fudge sauce

50g smooth peanut butter (I use Manilife)

1½ tablespoons cocoa powder (15g)

75g maple syrup

1 teaspoon soy sauce (or tamari)

1½ tablespoons water

Whipped yoghurt with roasted strawberries and peanut fudge sauce

The lime-roasted strawberries and peanut fudge sauce are essentially a refined combination of peanut butter and jelly, and boy do they sing together! Here I serve them with a simple whipped yoghurt, but you could serve with plain yoghurt or shop-bought ice cream. If you're feeling wild, pile the whipped yoghurt, roasted strawberries and fudge sauce on top of a caramelised roasted crumpet (page 236) and dust with cocoa powder to offset the sweetness.

———————

Preheat the oven to 200°C fan/220°C.

For the roasted strawberries, place all the ingredients in an ovenproof dish just big enough to fit the strawberries in a single layer. They should be snug, but not piled on top of each other. Bake for 20 minutes, stirring halfway, until the strawberries are very soft and have produced a bright red syrup. Set aside to cool.

Place the mascarpone, yoghurt, vanilla paste and maple syrup in a large bowl and whisk together until completely smooth. Keep the bowl in the fridge until ready to serve.

For the fudge sauce, whisk all the ingredients together in a small bowl until smooth. You may need to add more water or maple syrup, depending on the thickness of your peanut butter. You're looking for a smooth, thick but pourable consistency.

In individual glasses, layer the chilled yoghurt with the strawberries and the fudge sauce and serve.

Make ahead

The fudge sauce and strawberries will keep for 3 days refrigerated.

1 extra ripe pineapple, peeled and
        cut into 2cm-thick steaks
½ teaspoon caster sugar per steak,
        plus extra to serve
ground cinnamon, to serve

Maple custard

300g double cream, at room temperature
3 egg yolks, at room temperature
3 tablespoons maple syrup
½ teaspoon vanilla bean paste
a pinch of salt
optional: freshly grated nutmeg,
        ground cinnamon, tangerine
        or lemon zest

Make ahead

The custard will keep for up to 3 days in
the fridge. It will probably set in the fridge;
just reheat it very gently to get it back to
pouring consistency, adding a dash of
milk if needed.

Notes

Make sure you start with room temperature
pineapple. Cold pineapple will take much
longer to grill.

Pineapple steaks with maple custard

This is an extremely simple dessert that can be adjusted to serve however many
people you like. One regular pineapple will yield about 7 steaks, and you'll need
1–2 steaks per person, depending on appetite, so I'll leave you to do your own
personal pineapple maths. Make sure your pineapple is nice and ripe, otherwise it
won't caramelise as well.

I've never understood why so many custard recipes call for cornflour when
traditionally it's made without, and is so much better for it. I've always used a
simple combination of double cream, egg yolks and maple syrup, and the result is
incredibly quick and luxurious. Just remember the ratio 3:3:3 (300g cream,
3 egg yolks, 3 tablespoons of maple syrup), plus vanilla bean paste and a pinch
of salt, and you'll never have to look at another custard recipe again. You can also
add tangerine zest, freshly grated nutmeg, cinnamon or a bit of black pepper at
the end, to flavour your custard.

———————

Turn the oven grill to its highest setting.

Line a flat, sturdy tray with foil (a flimsy tray will warp under the heat of the grill
and produce uneven colouring). Arrange the pineapple steaks on the tray, a few
centimetres apart. Sprinkle each steak with ½ teaspoon of sugar.

Grill on the top shelf of the oven until browned and brûléed, about 8 minutes
but depending on the strength and heat of your oven grill, it could take anywhere
between 6 and 12 minutes, so keep an eye on them. You want them to look like
the picture! Turn the oven off and leave the steaks in the oven to soften in the
residual heat while you make the custard.

In a medium saucepan off the heat, whisk together the double cream, egg yolks,
maple syrup, vanilla and salt until completely smooth.

Place on a low heat (make sure you keep the heat low throughout) and cook,
stirring continuously with a spatula, for about 4 minutes for a loose, pourable
custard and 5–6 minutes for a thicker custard that will set when chilled. If your
custard is at all lumpy, just strain it through a sieve.

Sprinkle the steaks with a little sugar and cinnamon and serve with the custard.

Banana, sesame and maple cake

50g white sesame seeds (or start with
 toasted sesame seeds and skip
 the toasting), plus 1 teaspoon

70g melted ghee (from a jar not a tin,
 see page 17) or unsalted butter

90g soft light brown sugar

2 large eggs

60g ground almonds

30g plain flour (use gluten-free flour
 if you like)

1 teaspoon baking powder

¼ teaspoon fine salt

½ teaspoon vanilla bean paste

¼ teaspoon toasted sesame oil

2 teaspoons finely grated lemon zest

3–4 very ripe bananas, cut into
 2cm cubes (350g)

3 tablespoons maple syrup, plus extra
 to serve

½ teaspoon flaked salt

cold double cream, to serve

I'm a big fan of one-bowl cakes that don't require various elements to be mixed separately and then folded together. This cake is quite soft and pudding-y because of all the fruit, but it's complemented with crispy, sticky edges. It's easily gluten-free and relatively low in sugar, although that's neither here nor there.

The bananas you use should be very ripe and soft with black skins, if possible. Feel free to experiment with other soft, overripe fruits. Plums and pears work very well, for example. Serve with cold cream, a drizzle of maple syrup and preferably with coffee. Don't forget to sprinkle the cake with flaked sea salt.

———————

Preheat the oven to 180°C fan/200°C. Line a 20cm cake tin with non-stick parchment paper.

If starting with untoasted sesame seeds, spread the 50g of sesame seeds out on a baking tray and bake for 8–9 minutes, mixing a few times throughout, until golden-brown. Transfer the toasted seeds to a blender or spice grinder and grind to a coarse powder. Tip into a large mixing bowl.

Add the ghee, sugar, eggs, ground almonds, flour, baking powder, fine salt, vanilla, sesame oil and lemon zest and mix until fully combined. Fold in the bananas, trying not to crush the pieces, then spoon into the prepared tin.

Bake for 30 minutes, rotating the tin halfway so the cake colours evenly. After 30 minutes, drizzle over the maple syrup, sprinkle over the 1 teaspoon of sesame seeds and return to the oven for 10 minutes, until the surface is sticky and golden-brown and the edges are crispy.

Leave to cool for 20 minutes before releasing from the tin. Sprinkle with the flaked salt, then slice and serve warm with cold double cream and extra maple syrup drizzled on top. Remember, this is a moist cake owing to all the fruit. It doesn't have a traditional cake crumb and should be crispy on the outside and very soft on the inside.

Notes

To reheat, place slices on a tray in a cold oven, then turn the oven up to 150°C fan/170°C and warm for about 8 minutes.

SHOWSTOPPERS

Mango, basil and lime mille-feuille

Crunchy pastry

70g unsalted butter

90g spelt flour (you can also just
    use regular plain flour, or a mix
    of plain and wholemeal), plus extra
    for dusting

20g fine, quick-cook polenta
    (not the coarse variety that takes
    40 minutes to cook)

30g caster sugar

¼ teaspoon ground cinnamon

⅛ teaspoon fine salt

about 15 twists of freshly ground
    black pepper

1 tablespoon olive oil

40g ice-cold water

1 egg, whisked, for brushing the pastry

3 tablespoons demerara sugar

Mango

2 large, very ripe mangoes

2 teaspoons caster sugar

½ teaspoon vanilla bean paste

1 tablespoon lime juice

5g fresh basil leaves, plus 12 extra
    smaller leaves to serve

Ricotta cream

100g full-fat ricotta

70g double cream

50g extra-thick yoghurt

25g caster sugar

½ teaspoon vanilla bean paste

¼ teaspoon ground cinnamon

½ teaspoon finely grated lime zest

about 10 twists of freshly ground
    black pepper

I've rather hesitantly called this a 'mille-feuille' even though I know purists will be quick to tell me, quite correctly, that it's nothing like a traditional mille-feuille. The pastry here is crunchy from the polenta and the demerara sugar, rather than flaky. There is no custard, but instead a mix of ricotta, yoghurt and cream. And then there is fresh mango, which really can be interchanged with any seasonal fruit that pairs well with cinnamon and lime: cherries, plums, peaches and strawberries would all work beautifully. Make sure the fruit you're using – mango or otherwise – is soft, ripe and sweet. To make things easier, you can serve all the elements of the dessert in a bowl, rather than constructing them as per the picture. To make things easier still, you can serve the ricotta cream and macerated fruit with shop-bought biscuits, rather than making the pastry, which would make it a dessert worthy of a place in **QUICK FIXES**.

————————

Cut the butter into 2cm cubes and freeze for 15 minutes.

Put the flour, polenta, sugar, cinnamon, salt and pepper into a large bowl and stir together. Remove the butter from the freezer and add to the bowl along with the oil and water. Bring the pastry together until all the flour is incorporated but don't overwork it further.

Flour your surface, rolling pin and the dough. Tip the dough on to your surface and roll out to an A4-size rectangle. Fold the shorter ends of the pastry to meet in the middle, roll out, then fold the shorter sides in to meet in the middle again and roll out. Dust the pastry and your surface again if it's sticking, then fold the pastry in half, and roll out once more into a 15 x 10cm rectangle. Cover tightly with cling film and freeze for 30 minutes.

Flour your surface once more and roll the pastry out into a 4mm-thick 35x25cm rectangle. Flour the dough, surface and rolling pin as needed so the pastry doesn't stick. Carefully transfer to a large, flat, parchment-lined baking tray that will fit in your fridge, then refrigerate for 30 minutes.

Preheat the oven to 190°C fan/210°C.

Remove the pastry from the fridge and brush the egg all over. Sprinkle with the demerara sugar, pushing the sugar into the dough, then bake for 18–20 minutes, rotating the tray halfway, until golden-brown.

Continues on next page...

Mango, basil and lime mille-feuille continued...

The pastry will still be a little soft, but it will harden and become crunchy as it cools. Set aside to cool completely, then use a large, sharp knife to cut the pastry into 8 rectangles. Don't worry if they shatter a bit, this is a rustic dessert.

Peel the mangoes. Over a bowl, cut the flesh into random bite-size pieces, about 8mm thick. Add the sugar, vanilla, lime juice and basil and gently stir together. Add more sugar and lime to taste if your mango isn't particularly juicy and sweet. Leave to macerate for at least 20 minutes (or up to 3 hours). Remove the basil before assembling/serving.

Put all the ingredients for the ricotta cream into a medium bowl. With a whisk, whip the cream vigorously until thickened into medium peaks, 1–2 minutes.

To assemble, place 4 of the pastry rectangles on a flat tray. Cover each with a good amount of ricotta cream, followed by a few slices of the mango and some of its syrup. Top with another rectangle of pastry, then spoon over more cream, mango and syrup. Finish with the small fresh basil leaves and serve. NB: you'll see in the picture that there are 3 layers, which I'll admit we did for aesthetic purposes. In terms of portion size, 2 layers is quite enough per person.

Get ahead
The pastry will keep in the fridge for up to 3 days, and in the freezer forever. Make sure it's wrapped up tightly in cling film.

125g savoiardi biscuits

Roasted strawberries

550g strawberries, green tops
    removed, large strawberries
    quartered and smaller ones halved
    (you'll need 900g strawberries in
    total for this recipe, see below)
100g caster sugar
½ teaspoon vanilla bean paste
½ lime, halved
4 cinnamon sticks (15g)

Chipotle chocolate ganache

200g double cream
90g dark cooking chocolate
40g milk cooking chocolate
¼ teaspoon chilli flakes
½ teaspoon chipotle flakes (optional)
a good pinch of salt

Fresh strawberries

350g strawberries, green tops removed
15g caster sugar
2 limes: 2 teaspoons finely grated lime zest
    and 1½ tablespoons juice

Cinnamon cream

200g double cream
2 large good-quality egg yolks
2 tablespoons maple syrup
1½ tablespoons ground cinnamon
a pinch of salt

Notes

The layer cake needs to set overnight,
or for at least 12 hours.

Make ahead

Roast the strawberries and make the
cinnamon cream the day before.

Strawberry, cinnamon and chipotle chocolate layer cake

Every year on our birthday, my mother makes my sister and me the same cake, based on a cake she once had in Rio. It has four layers, repeated: whipped cream, crushed strawberries, *biscoitos champanhe* (savoiardi biscuits) and dark chocolate. Sounds pretty good, right? Right! But let me give you a little context. My mum is not the most enthusiastic cook (don't worry, she knows this and won't berate me for being factual). Not only that, but she is also, quite possibly, the healthiest person in the world. She's a nutritionist with an intolerance to gluten (and soy, preservatives, processed oils) and no gallbladder, which basically means she can't eat many delicious things.

So what's the healthiest person in the world doing making a cake laced with not only dairy and gluten, but also sugar? Well, the short answer is that she makes it because it's incredibly easy and involves no baking, and she doesn't eat any of it, anyway. She keeps it very simple, with unembellished layers of whipped cream and crushed strawberries (no added sugar, of course), *biscoitos champanhe* and melted dark chocolate.

My family and I have come to find comfort in this no-bake, low-sugar tradition. Of course, I've had to go and complicate things by making a very fancy version of what is supposed to be a very simple dessert. I've added a layer of roasted strawberries laced with cinnamon and lime, a layer of soft whipped cinnamon cream, a layer of chipotle chocolate ganache (for goodness sake!). My mother was pretty exasperated when I told her about it, but I'm confident you'll enjoy the fanciness. It's an epic showstopper of a dessert that is very much worth the effort.

Preheat the oven to 200°C fan/220°C. Line a large 900g loaf tin (or a similar-sized dish) with cling film, so it drapes over the sides.

For the roasted strawberries, place the strawberries, sugar, vanilla, lime and cinnamon in a 30cm baking dish and mix well. Don't crowd the strawberries into a smaller pan as they need to cook in a single layer or the resulting syrup will be too thin and runny. Roast for 25–30 minutes, stirring halfway, until the strawberries are soft and the liquid is the consistency of maple syrup. Leave to cool. Discard the lime and cinnamon sticks.

Continues on page 256...

Strawberry, cinnamon and chipotle chocolate layer cake continued...

For the ganache, put the cream into a medium saucepan and place on a medium-low heat. Warm for 2 minutes or until gently steaming, then remove from the heat and add all the chocolate, chilli, chipotle and salt, but don't mix yet. After a few minutes, whisk the chocolate into the cream until completely smooth. Leave to cool completely.

For the fresh strawberries, put the strawberries, sugar, lime zest and lime juice into a food processor or blender and pulse to get a rough mash. Don't overwork, you don't want a purée. If you don't have a processor, use a potato masher.

For the cinnamon cream, put the cream, egg yolks, maple syrup, cinnamon and salt into the bowl of a stand mixer with the whisk attachment in place and whip to get medium peaks, 4½–6 minutes on medium-high speed.

Once the roasted strawberries and ganache have cooled completely (and not before!), layer the dessert in the lined tin in this order, smoothing the top of each layer as you go so they're even:

All the roasted strawberries and their syrup
Half the biscuits
Two-thirds of the fresh strawberries
All the cinnamon cream
All the ganache
The remaining half of the biscuits
The remaining third of the fresh strawberries

Cover with cling film and refrigerate overnight or for at least 12 hours.

When you're ready to serve, place a platter on top of the tin and quickly flip the whole thing over. Give the tin a good tap all over to release the dessert, then lift off the tin and peel away the cling film. Serve at once, returning any leftovers to the fridge immediately.

Peach and rooibos iced tea sorbet

600g soft, ripe yellow peaches (nectarines
or apricots would also work well)

100g caster sugar

50g water

5 rooibos tea bags

2 lemons: 3 strips of peel and
4 tablespoons of juice

1 tablespoon vodka, gin or tequila
(optional, but this will help keep
the sorbet smooth)

When I think about the flavours of my childhood in Italy, there's perhaps nothing more nostalgic than peach iced tea, specifically Estha Thé. Never from a bottle and always from those snap-apart plastic cartons with foil lids that you puncture with sharp little straws. Esta Thé was pretty much a daily feature for *merenda* (the afternoon snack Italian kids have after school), and there was nothing more delicious and thirst-quenching in the blistering heat of summer.

I still love peach iced tea, but these days I make it myself, so I can dictate how sweet I want it to be, and also so I can zhuzh it up. Instead of black tea, I like to use rooibos tea, which is native to South Africa and has a beautifully floral and honey-like flavour.

Make sure your peaches are soft, sweet and ripe – underripe fruit just won't cut it here. Feel free to experiment with other ripe, seasonal fruits: apricots or plums work really well, for example.

———————

Halve the peaches, then remove the stones. Chop the flesh into 2cm pieces, leaving the skin on – you should have 500g. Transfer to a wide container or a tray that will fit into the freezer and freeze for 3 hours, or until frozen solid.

Meanwhile, put the sugar and water in a small saucepan. Place on a medium heat until the sugar dissolves and the mixture begins to gently bubble, about 2 minutes. Remove from the heat and add the tea bags, lemon peel, lemon juice and the alcohol (or 1 tablespoon of water). Stir together, then leave to infuse until the syrup is completely cool. Squeeze the tea bags into the syrup – really make sure you get all the liquid out, then discard the tea bags.

Once the peaches have frozen solid, put them into a large food processor with the cooled syrup and the lemon peel. Blitz until completely smooth, scraping down the sides every now and then. If using a blender, add all the syrup and only a quarter of the peaches to the blender to begin with. Blitz until completely smooth before adding the rest of the peaches and blending until smooth.

Transfer to a wide container, smoothing the top. Seal and freeze for 1½ hours before serving, or until set but still scoopable. You can also serve straight after blitzing, but the sorbet will be quite soft.

Serves 6

Miso caramel ice cream bomba

Miso caramel ice cream

380g double cream, at least 45% fat
content, fridge cold (light, single
and whipping cream won't work here)

3 large, good-quality egg yolks

90g maple syrup

30g white miso paste

1½ teaspoons vanilla bean paste

Miso caramel brittle

80g roasted and salted peanuts or
roasted and salted almonds

140g maple syrup

70g double cream

25g white miso paste

1 teaspoon vanilla bean paste

Chocolate shell

140g dark cooking chocolate

60g milk cooking chocolate

2 tablespoons coconut oil

To serve

1–2 tablespoons cocoa, for dusting

Notes

I've divided the ingredients list with
subheadings for clarity, but please note
that some of the main ingredients feature
throughout the recipe. You'll need a total
of 450g of double cream, 230g of maple
syrup, 55g of white miso paste and 2½
teaspoons of vanilla bean paste.

A *bomba di gelato* – ice cream bomb – is essentially just ice cream set in a large bowl. As a child in Italy, this was my favourite way of eating gelato, undoubtedly because of the size and drama of the presentation.

This dessert features three elements – an ice cream, a caramel and a chocolate topping – which all need time freezing and chilling. You'll definitely need to start the day before you plan to eat it, but I'd highly recommend starting 2 days ahead, that way you can finish the whole thing the day before, and just casually whip it out of the freezer – ta dah! – when you're ready to serve.

Having said all that, you absolutely don't have to construct a bomba if you're more interested in just eating the damn thing sooner rather than later. For a simpler version, make the ice cream and freeze until set. Scoop into serving glasses, drizzle over the chocolate shell and finish with chunks of the caramel brittle.

Don't be tempted to whip all the ice cream ingredients together from the get-go. If you add the miso too early, the cream will split (unlike the Coffee ice cream on page 266, for which you can whip all the ice cream ingredients at the same time).

———————

Line a 1.2-litre capacity bowl (that's a medium-sized bowl – mine was 18cm wide and 19cm tall) with two layers of cling film, so that it drapes over the sides. Alternatively use a loaf tin.

For the ice cream, put the (chilled) cream and egg yolks into the bowl of a stand mixer with the whisk attachment in place. Whip on high speed until thickened into medium peaks the consistency of loose soft-serve ice cream. This usually takes about 3 minutes but could take up to 6 minutes depending on the fat content of the cream you're using. In a small bowl, whisk together the maple syrup, miso and vanilla until completely smooth, then fold this mixture through the cream until fully incorporated. Spoon into the prepared bowl and smooth the top to make sure it's level. Cover tightly with foil and freeze overnight, or until frozen through.

The next day, start the caramel brittle. Preheat the oven to 170°C fan/190°C. Once the oven is hot, spread the peanuts on a flat tray and roast for 6 minutes, or until deeply golden-brown (although the peanuts are already roasted and salted, most shop-bought varieties are still quite pale and frankly not roasted long enough, hence the extra roast). If you're using roasted salted almonds, you shouldn't need to roast them again. Once cool, roughly chop the nuts.

Continues on next page...

Miso caramel ice cream bomba continued...

Place the maple syrup, double cream, miso and vanilla bean paste in a medium saucepan on a medium heat. Cook for 6 minutes, stirring often; the mixture should bubble away and thicken to the consistency of a thick butterscotch sauce. Transfer to a bowl, stir in the nuts, then set aside until completely cool.

Remove the ice cream bowl from the freezer. Spoon the thick, nutty caramel on to the ice cream, smoothing it out to evenly cover the surface (if the caramel has set relatively hard, this might be easiest with your hands). Cover loosely with foil and return to the freezer for another 4 hours.

After 4 hours (or the next day), make the chocolate top layer. Put the chocolate and coconut oil into a bowl and set over a pan of gently simmering water. Once most of the chocolate has melted, remove from the heat and stir until completely smooth. Set aside until the chocolate has cooled completely but is still liquid.

Remove the ice cream bowl from the freezer and leave to stand for 5 minutes. Place a wire rack over the bowl, then quickly flip the whole thing over so the bomba ends up on the rack.

Place the rack on a tray, remove the bowl and then carefully peel off the cling film. Pour the cooled chocolate evenly over the bomba to cover it, working quickly because the chocolate will solidify as soon as it touches the cold ice cream. Dust the surface with cocoa powder, then leave for about 5 minutes, or until the chocolate has set hard.

Use a large spatula to carefully transfer the bomba to a large plate. Refrigerate for 5 minutes, or until the chocolate is completely hard. If making ahead, store the bomba in the freezer, and take it out 15–20 minutes before serving, so the ice cream softens.

Use a large, sharp knife dipped in hot water to crack through the shell and cut large slices of the bomba. There's almost no way the slices will be neat, but there's absolutely nothing wrong with that.

Serves 6

Base

200g ginger nut biscuits (or a mix
    of ginger nut and hard amaretti)

80g coconut oil, melted

¾ teaspoon ground ginger

¾ teaspoon ground cinnamon

¼ teaspoon fine salt

Chocolate ganache

400g tin of full-fat coconut milk
    (at least 70% coconut extract)

300g dark cooking chocolate,
    roughly chopped (or a mix of dark
    and milk chocolate)

3 tablespoons maple syrup (if using
    milk chocolate you might not need
    any, add to taste)

½ teaspoon vanilla bean paste

a pinch of flaked salt

To serve

2 teaspoons cocoa powder

After dinner chocolate tart

I hate it when people say, 'This is all I want in a ...' but really, this is all I want in a dessert. I'm not one to order anything rich or creamy after a big dinner because all I ever really want is a hit of chocolate. This is a hit, and then some!

As long as you use dairy-free chocolate, this tart is completely vegan. I'm not vegan, so I like to use a mix of two-thirds dark chocolate and one-third milk chocolate in the ganache, and a mix of ginger nut biscuits and hard amaretti biscuits in the base. The recipe will also work just as well with double cream instead of coconut milk, if that's what you have. Tangerine or orange zest and chipotle chilli flakes are a lovely addition to the ganache, if you feel like something a little more adventurous.

It's really important that the coconut milk you use has a fat content of at least 70%, otherwise the tart won't set properly. Use coconut cream instead, if you can't find coconut milk with a high enough fat content.

The tart needs to set in the fridge for at least 5 hours.

———

Line the base and sides of a 20cm cake tin with a removable base with non-stick parchment.

For the base, put the biscuits into a food processor and blitz until fully combined into a coarse crumb. If you don't have a food processor, bash the biscuits in a bag with a rolling pin to get a coarse crumb. Transfer to a bowl with the melted coconut oil, spices and salt and mix to combine.

Transfer to the prepared tin and press down firmly to create an even, compacted layer.

For the ganache filling, whisk the coconut milk in a medium saucepan on a medium-high heat, then cook for a couple of minutes until steaming. Remove from the heat and add the chocolate, maple syrup, vanilla and flaked salt (and some tangerine zest and a pinch of chipotle chilli flakes, if you like). Set aside for a few minutes, then whisk until completely smooth. Leave to cool for 15 minutes.

Pour the ganache on to the base, then refrigerate for at least 5 hours but preferably overnight, until the ganache is completely set.

Remove from the fridge, then, while still in the tin, dust the surface with the cocoa powder. Release the tart from the tin, then transfer to a platter and serve.

Coffee ice cream with Kahlua fudge sauce

Ice cream

300g double cream (at least
    45% fat), fridge cold

90g maple syrup

50g dark or milk chocolate,
    roughly grated

2 good-quality egg yolks

1½ tablespoons instant coffee
    powder (if you have granules,
    blitz to a powder first)

2 teaspoons ground filter coffee

1½ teaspoons vanilla bean paste

1½ teaspoons cocoa powder

⅛ teaspoon flaked salt

Kahlua fudge sauce

90g tahini (mix very well before using,
    to combine the solids and fat)

60g Kahlua (or sweetened espresso)

40g maple syrup

2 tablespoon cocoa powder

1½ teaspoons soy sauce or tamari

½ teaspoon vanilla bean paste

Coconut flakes (optional)

80g dried coconut flakes

60g maple syrup

1 teaspoon ground filter coffee

¼ teaspoon flaked salt

about 8 twists of freshly ground
    black pepper

Notes

For a caffeine-free chocolate version,
replace the coffee powder and grounds
with the same amount of cocoa powder.

I've never excelled at making proper ice cream from scratch; it involves too much time and too many processes, and I'll be honest – I'm quite lazy when it comes to desserts. Proper ice cream involves making a crème anglaise base: tempering yolks with milk and cream that has likely been infused overnight, then churning and freezing the mixture.

When it comes to complicated desserts, I often find myself trying to work out ways of getting great results in half the time. Enter this ice cream, in which all the ingredients are put into the bowl of a stand mixer at the same time and whipped together before freezing. No infusing, no tempering, no churning – and yet the results are incredibly smooth.

I posted a version of this recipe to my Instagram a couple of summers ago, and it went down a storm. This one is better yet, with yolks instead of whites, and with the addition of flecks of chocolate throughout. I've said it before and I'll say it again – I'd offer a money-back guarantee to go with my claim that this is one of the easiest and best ice creams you'll ever make.

———————

For the ice cream, place all the ingredients in the bowl of a stand mixer. With the whisk attachment, whip on high speed for 3–6 minutes, or until thickened to medium peaks/the texture of loose, soft-serve ice cream. Transfer to a wide container, smoothing the top. Seal and freeze for 1 hour.

For the fudge sauce, put all the ingredients into a medium bowl and whisk until thickened and completely smooth.

After 1 hour, remove the ice cream from the freezer and swirl in two-thirds of the fudge sauce to get streaks. Seal and return to the freezer until set, 3–4 hours.

If making the coconut flakes, preheat the oven to 160°C fan/180°C.

On a parchment-lined baking tray, mix all the ingredients for the coconut flakes together so they are fully coated, then spread out as much as possible. Bake for 16–18 minutes, or until crisp and deeply golden-brown.

Serve the ice cream with the coconut flakes sprinkled on top, and the remaining fudge sauce on the side. The consistency is best after about 4 hours of freezing. Once it has frozen solid, defrost in the fridge for 15–20 minutes before serving.

100g caster sugar

5 large passion fruits

397g tin of condensed milk

320g whole milk (semi-skimmed
    won't work)

1½ teaspoons finely grated tangerine zest

¼ teaspoon chilli flakes
    (optional, leave out completely
    or just add a pinch if you prefer)

2 large eggs, plus 1 extra yolk

1 teaspoon vanilla bean paste

a pinch of fine salt

Passion fruit pudim

All over Brazil, there are buffet-style restaurants called 'kilos' where you pay for your food by weight. Most of these are cheapish restaurants, but not when you're as greedy as me. My mother has always said that 'my eyes are bigger than my stomach' and she's not wrong, so you can imagine just how excited I get whenever I'm in a kilo. I go IN. What is perhaps slightly more surprising is the fact that I go overboard on desserts as well as savouries, which is very unlike me (I don't usually order dessert unless coerced by whoever I'm dining with). Pudim de leite condensado – which is essentially a slightly thicker and less wobbly flan made with condensed milk, features on every dessert counter in every kilo in the land, I would hazard, and it was always the dessert I headed for first. My favourite kilo in Rio always had a big platter of halved passion fruits on ice on the dessert counter, which I would scoop out and spoon over my pudim, and that's how this recipe was born.

———————

Preheat the oven to 170°C (no fan).

Have a round 20cm ovenproof dish or tin ready. Make sure the dish/tin doesn't have a removable base, or else your caramel will escape.

Sprinkle the sugar evenly into a medium non-stick frying pan and place on a medium heat. Gently cook for 5–6 minutes, swirling the pan once the sugar begins to melt. Keep cooking until the sugar has liquified and turned from light amber to dark amber. Watch the pan closely – you need to remove it from the heat as soon as it turns a darker shade of amber, or it could easily burn. Pour the caramel into your dish/tin and swirl it to evenly coat the base. Set aside while you make the custard.

Scoop the pulp from the passion fruits – you want 90g of pulp.

Put the passion fruit pulp into a large bowl with the condensed milk, whole milk, tangerine zest, chilli flakes, eggs, yolk, vanilla and a pinch of salt. Gently whisk until combined. Don't whisk too vigorously, as you want to avoid creating air bubbles.

Tap the caramel to make sure it has set hard. Place the pudim dish in a large, high-sided baking tray. Pour the custard through a sieve into the pudim dish and then discard the solids.

Continues on next page...

Make ahead

Make the dessert at least the day before you plan to serve it, or up to 3 days ahead.

Passion fruit pudim continued...

Place the baking tray on the middle shelf of the oven. Pour hot (not boiling) water into the larger tin to come halfway up the sides of the pudim dish. Bake for 45 minutes, until set on top but still wobbly. Remove from the oven and leave the pudim to cool for 1 hour before removing from the water bath and refrigerating overnight.

Remove the pudim from the fridge 10 minutes before you want to serve it. Run a knife around the edges of the pudim to release it. Place a large, lipped platter on top of the tin, then quickly flip the whole thing over. Gently lift off the tin – the pudim should have released itself on to the plate, but if not, give the tin a good bang on the top and sides. Slice, and serve.

Serves 4

45g caster sugar (if making crème brûlée)

crème fraîche, to serve (if serving as
    set custard)

Chocolate layer

25g cocoa powder, plus extra to serve

1½ tablespoons maple syrup

40g hot espresso or very strong coffee

a pinch of salt

Custard

300g double cream, at room temperature

3 large good-quality egg yolks,
    at room temperature

3 tablespoons maple syrup

½ teaspoon vanilla bean paste

a pinch of salt

½ teaspoon ground cinnamon

Cinnamon custard brûlée

This dessert features cinnamon custard with a surprise chocolate layer beneath it. You have two options here: either serve as a cheat's crème brûlée, a quick(er) version of the classic dessert that involves no tempering of egg yolks and no bain-marie, but to achieve that cracking sugar crust, you'll need a blowtorch. Alternatively, if you don't have a blowtorch (or if you want a less sweet dessert), you can simply dust the tops of the pots with cocoa powder, and serve with a spoonful of crème fraîche.

These will need to set overnight, so start the day before.

———

First make the chocolate layer. In a small bowl, whisk together the cocoa powder, maple syrup and hot coffee until smooth. Spoon into four ramekins or small bowls, or pour it all into one larger dish. Refrigerate while you make the custard.

In a medium saucepan off the heat, whisk together the double cream, egg yolks, maple syrup, vanilla bean paste and salt.

Place on a low heat (make sure you keep the heat low throughout) and cook, stirring continuously with a spatula, for 6–10 minutes, or until you get a thick custard. If your custard is at all lumpy, just strain it through a sieve.

Set aside to cool for 5 minutes, then stir in the cinnamon. Leave to cool for 20 minutes, then pour the custard into the ramekins, on top of the set chocolate layer. Tap the ramekins on the work surface to level them out, then refrigerate uncovered for at least 4 hours, or preferably overnight, until set.

If you're brûléeing, sprinkle each ramekin with 1½ teaspoons of sugar. Place the ramekins on a metal tray and use a blowtorch on high to melt the sugar evenly until it caramelises and hardens. Leave to set for 5 minutes before serving.

Alternatively, if you don't have a blowtorch, dust the surface of each ramekin with cocoa powder, and top with a spoonful of crème fraîche.

Coconut, chocolate and coffee roll

Dough

210g '00' flour

4g fast-action dried yeast

30g soft light brown sugar

1 teaspoon vanilla bean paste

1 teaspoon finely grated tangerine
   (or orange) zest

1 teaspoon finely grated lemon zest

¼ teaspoon fine salt

130g lukewarm water

olive oil, for greasing

Coconut glaze

90g creamed coconut (I use Tropical
   Sun, from a 200g packet)

120g full-fat coconut milk from a tin,
   (at least 70% coconut extract)

110g icing sugar

¾ teaspoon white miso paste

¼ teaspoon flaked salt

Filling

50g dark chocolate, roughly grated
   or very finely chopped

¾ teaspoon ground cinnamon,
   plus extra to serve

¾ teaspoon instant coffee granules,
   plus extra to serve

Wash

½ tablespoon plant-based or dairy milk

½ tablespoon olive oil

1 tablespoon soft light brown sugar

Notes

Creamed coconut is not the same as coconut cream. It usually comes in a small, 200g cardboard box, sometimes in a jar, but never in a tin. Creamed coconut is made from the dehydrated pulp of coconut and so it is sweeter, more intensely coconutty and more textured than coconut milk, coconut cream or coconut oil.

The star of the show here is the dough. Flavoured with vanilla, tangerine zest and lemon zest, it's vegan and incredibly versatile. It can be used as it is here, or deep-fried into donuts. This giant, sticky roll is entirely vegan but honestly, you'd never know it. It's more of an afternoon treat, perfect with coffee, rather than a dessert. Feel free to switch up the filling and glaze by experimenting with different jams, nut butters and chocolates.

———

Preheat the oven to the very lowest temperature (no higher than 50°C).

Put all the ingredients for the dough into the bowl of a stand mixer with a dough hook attached and knead on medium-high speed for 10 minutes. If you don't have a mixer, bring the ingredients together in a bowl, then transfer to a work surface dusted with flour and knead for 15 minutes, dusting with more flour as needed. The resulting dough should be smooth, pliable and slightly sticky.

Turn the oven off.

Tip the dough on to a clean work surface. Lightly grease your mixing bowl with olive oil. Shape the dough into a smooth, round mass and return it to the bowl. Lightly grease the surface of the dough with olive oil to stop it drying out, then cover the bowl with a damp cloth. Place the bowl in the switched-off oven and leave to prove for 1 hour, or until doubled in size.

Meanwhile, make the coconut glaze. Place the contents of the 200g packet of creamed coconut in a bowl and place over a pan of gently simmering water. Once melted and softened, mix everything together to combine the solids and fat. Measure out 90g into a separate bowl and store the rest in a sealed jar for another recipe. Once the creamed coconut has cooled completely, add the coconut milk, icing sugar, miso and flaked salt and whisk until fully combined.

Place a large piece of non-stick parchment paper on your work surface and lightly grease it with olive oil.

Tip the proved dough on to your oily paper. Use your hands to stretch the dough out into a 34 x 24cm rectangle – the dough will spring back at first, but keep on stretching it into a rectangle until it stops springing back. Try to make sure the thickness of the dough is relatively even, and patch up any holes that form by pinching the dough back together.

Continues on next page...

Coconut, chocolate and coffee roll continued...

Spread half the coconut glaze evenly all over the dough. Mix the chocolate, cinnamon and coffee granules together then sprinkle evenly over to cover the glaze. Starting at the shorter end, use the parchment paper to help you roll the dough up into a Swiss roll. Once rolled it should be seam side down. Tuck the dough in and under at either end, to stop the filling escaping. Use the parchment to help you lift the roll on to a flat baking tray.

Leave to prove, uncovered, for another 40 minutes. Preheat the oven to 180°C fan/200°C.

Mix the milk and oil together for the wash. Brush the roll all over with the milk mixture, then evenly sprinkle over 1 tablespoon of sugar. Once the oven is hot, bake the roll for 25 minutes, rotating the tray halfway so it colours evenly.

Leave to rest for 30 minutes, or until completely cool to the touch (otherwise the glaze will melt). Once cool, spoon the remaining coconut glaze over the roll, letting it drip over the sides. Finish with a sprinkle of flaked salt, coffee granules and cinnamon. Slice and serve.